"*Learning to Be Literate: More Than a Single Story* reminds us that prototypical children do not exist and that the joys of teaching are deeply connected to the individual, unique, and always amazing children that fill our classrooms. Paugh and MacPhee challenge media-driven messages about how children learn to read without entering the reading wars or the fray of polemical debates. Instead, they draw on the best of reading scholarship to share what we know about teaching young children to read, write, and become literate citizens. This text is filled with real-life strategies and teaching scenarios for everything from phonemic awareness to critical literacy, and is certain to be a valuable resource for every teacher."

—**Catherine Compton-Lilly**, John C. Hungerpiller Professor, University of South Carolina–Columbia

"*Learning to Be Literate* is a thoughtful, engaging, and persuasive text that acknowledges the relevance of 'skills' in literacy instruction while firmly situating literacy learning in the context of meaningful reading and writing—and always taking into account students' lived experiences. But what stands out is the respect Paugh and MacPhee show for children as competent learners and teachers as knowledgeable professionals. This text will be an invaluable addition to any primary teacher's professional library."

—**Curt Dudley-Marling**, professor emeritus, Boston College

"*Learning to Be Literate* offers an antidote to the venom surrounding the historical and contemporary debates around reading and literacy instruction. Paugh and MacPhee's organizing framework challenges us to think beyond simple views by respecting interdisciplinary contributions to how we understand and teach for literacy. The classroom vignettes make the concepts real, the connections to families are critical, and the authors' clear regard for children and their teachers shines through."

—**C. Patrick Proctor**, professor, Lynch School of Education & Human Development, Boston College

"With the resurgence of the 'reading wars,' including false dichotomies of phonics and meaning-based literacy instruction, the time for this book is now. Building on recent research and theoretical insights in the learning sciences, Paugh and MacPhee invite readers to consider multiple pathways toward becoming literate to support the diverse strengths and needs of their students. This is a must-read for new and experienced teachers alike!"

—**Lara J. Handsfield**, PhD, professor of elementary literacy and bilingual education, Illinois State University

"*Learning to Be Literate: More Than a Single Story* is a timely and long overdue book that strikes a perfect balance between theories of literacy learning and practical classroom applications. Through the Active Literacy Learning (ALL) framework, Paugh and MacPhee provide compelling arguments on why taking a single view of literacy learning can be detrimental to creating inclusive learning environments. *Learning to Be Literate* is a must-read for early literacy educators who support students to be, first and foremost, agents in their own learning."

—**Bobbie Kabuto**, PhD, interim dean, School of Education, Queens College, City University of New York

learning
to be
literate

NORTON BOOKS IN EDUCATION

learning
to be
literate

More Than a Single Story

Patricia Paugh • Deborah MacPhee

Foreword by Rachael Gabriel

Norton Professional Books

An Imprint of W. W. Norton & Company
Celebrating a Century of Independent Publishing

Note to Readers: *Learning to Be Literate* is intended as a general information resource for professionals practicing in the field of education. It is not a substitute for appropriate training. No technique or recommendation is guaranteed to be effective in all circumstances, and neither the publisher nor the author can guarantee the complete accuracy, efficacy, or appropriateness of any recommendation in every respect.

The names and potentially identifying characteristics of certain individuals and organizations have been changed and some characters and organizations are composites. Also, some dialogue and scenarios have been reconstructed and some are composites.

Any URLs displayed in this book link or refer to websites that existed as of press time. The publisher is not responsible for, and should not be deemed to endorse or recommend, any website, app, or other content that it did not create. The author, also, is not responsible for any third-party material.

For information about permission to reproduce selections from this book, write to Permissions, W. W. Norton & Company, Inc., 500 Fifth Avenue, New York, NY 10110

For information about special discounts for bulk purchases, please contact W. W. Norton Special Sales at specialsales@wwnorton.com or 800-233-4830

Manufacturing by Versa Press
Production manager: Gwen Cullen

ISBN: 978-1-324-02001-1 (pbk)

W. W. Norton & Company, Inc., 500 Fifth Avenue, New York, NY 10110
www.wwnorton.com

W. W. Norton & Company Ltd., 15 Carlisle Street, London W1D 3BS

1 2 3 4 5 6 7 8 9 0

For three who inspire me as a literacy educator:
My brother Joseph, my grandson James, and my granddaughter Ella

—PP

For Mom and Dad,
and for all the children I have had the privilege to teach
—DM

Contents

Acknowledgments

Our names are listed as the authors of this book, but it is the accumulation of the wisdom of mentors, colleagues, and students who pushed our wondering about what knowledge is important in the teaching of literacy. We are indebted to mentors Curt Dudley-Marling, Lara Handsfield, and the late John Gorman, who valued our participation in this conversation and who encouraged our growth as researchers and writers. The original framing of this text grew from initial investigations into discourses around early reading research and instruction with many colleagues in our professional circles, with special recognition to Sherry Sanden.

We also wish to thank the many teachers and students who have invited us into their classrooms to learn with and from them across the years. We are especially indebted to those who invited us back time and again, engaging with us in collaborative dialogue, research, and scholarly writing, including Mary Moran, Morgan Belcher, Shannon Crawford, and Stacey Waugh.

At this point in time, priceless recognition has been earned by patient family members who probably know more about reading and writing than they ever thought possible. Thank you Fonda Proctor, Jim Paugh III, Jim Paugh IV, and Nicola Paugh. Additionally, this book would not be published without the expert eye and deep confidence in our work from our editor Carol Collins, the graphic design talents of Bentley Brown, and the editorial support of Hudson Perrigo and Mariah Eppes.

Finally, we owe a huge debt of gratitude to all who have shown us that learning to be literate is indeed more than a single story, including preservice teachers who have shared and reflected on their literacy histories in course assignments; parents who have communicated trials and triumphs as they inquire about how best to support their children as readers and writers; and the children themselves, who have included us in their stories, teaching us who they are and how we can teach and inspire them to become skilled and competent users of literacy. The children are our inspiration.

Foreword

Learning to Be Literate arrives at a moment when historic debates about early literacy instruction have entered the accelerated age of the internet and social media. Discussions and disagreements that used to unfold over weeks and months in books and articles, or television and newspapers, are now carried out moment-by-moment in social media, podcasts, listservs, and documentaries. This has created more chatter, more distractions, and fewer trustworthy sources of information; it is increasingly common to assume that everyone and everything is suspect and has taken a side.

Since the 1990s, state and federal legislation has aimed to ensure that the quality of early reading instruction is universally high by mandating standards-based, research-based, evidence-based, and—most recently—science of reading-based instruction.

Such categories are meant to clarify what is good or right from what is not, but they rarely do. They function in the same way that food labels might, with "all natural" or "farm fresh" seeming to indicate what is wholesome, without any guarantee. They are used as shorthand for a range of ideas and approaches by a range of individuals whose intended meaning grows increasingly unclear as the concepts and related conversations shift and change over time.

As often happens across history, debates about early reading instruction are about more than reading instruction. They are an expression of underlying anxieties and uncertainties about some of the outcomes of literacy: identity, economic health, community, and safety. One could argue that disagreements over the nature and shape of early literacy instruction never really go away; rather, they gain more or less traction depending on a number of factors—including, but not limited to, how optimistic people are about the economy, society, and public institutions.

As these indicators of stability vary, so do confidence, clarity, and insight about early literacy instruction. Insight in particular suffers because of the time spent explaining, defining, defending, rebranding, and retraining instead of investigating, improving, and refining. We all wonder what might break the cycle. This is exactly where Paugh and MacPhee lead us.

At a time when it is common to talk about culturally responsive pedagogy *or* the science of reading; multilingual learners *or* the neuroscience of reading; neurodiversity *or* phonics instruction, Paugh and MacPhee's framework invites us to fully engage the multidimensional nature of literacy, the natural and divine diversity of human people, and the synergy in learning environments that can be achieved when these multiple variables meet. They do so not only by sharing a clear-eyed vision of what literacy instruction can be, but by framing, illustrating, and demonstrating it within and across each of their chapters.

We meet the authors in the first pages: from their own literacy histories, their memories of becoming educators, their families, mentors, favorite writers. We learn that "becoming literate" requires being literate in different ways over time, and that it requires community: both human and textual. We all have experiences in the company of writers and thinkers. We read their words, write with them in mind, and talk about their ideas.

We also have experiences in the company of the humans we live and work among. We read, write, and talk with them. Their influences are part of our development as people in the same way favorite books and authors shape our consciousnesses, preferences, and ideals. They position us, and, at best, remind us of who we are and who we could be.

Considering multiple ways of being literate reminds us to consider each human as, in some ways, always, already literate: working to increase understanding and control in each of the communities and endeavors they choose or encounter. This understanding creates the possibility of presuming competence and potential in every learner, even and especially those for whom school is not an easy or comfortable fit.

More than creating a conceptual space for all kinds of minds, the authors provide a practical framework for creating and adjusting instruction in schools for students They argue for diversity in learning experiences as a way to widen the welcome for all kinds of minds, learners, and literate beings at different places in their growth and development, and they provide specific illustrations of what that could look like and why it matters. The universality of difference requires that we design for diversity, and yet so many of school's taken-for-granted structures and processes are designed for sameness and compliance.

These authors know early literacy well—as educators, scholars, parent, and citizens; both what it has been, and what it could be. Following their lead means not being seduced by simplicity or drawn in by narrow understandings that seem to make quick work of complex processes. It means knowing that literacy is human and thus, by necessity, multidimensional. It means acknowledging that literacy instruction that is not likewise multidimensional is always, quite simply, missing something. And it means remembering the personal in the political, the individual in the average, and the potential in each person. This widens opportunities for those who have traditionally been marginalized, and who have struggled in school settings, and also for those whose ways of being and doing school have always been viewed as literate and have always somehow fit. Classrooms do not have to resemble a normal distribution where some are ahead and others behind, some are successful and others not, some fit and others don't. They can be better than that. They can be sites of liberation, of discovery, and of self-actualization.

Paugh and MacPhee's multidimensional framework unites what cognitive science, cultural studies, and social psychology have offered in isolation, as ways of understanding learning and growth, and creates a rising tide of possibility that has the potential to lift all learners—along with their teachers. After all, an educator's ability to design for diversity newly empowers them to reach their own full potential as well. What follows between the covers of this book is unlike any other text on teaching beginning reading. It is practical without being didactic and invites you to dream without being too abstract. It is a text we need because of its integration of dimensions, ideas, and discourses that too often echo in their social media silos without this rare opportunity to harmonize. The idea of harmony captures the possibility and power in complexity, in more than one thing being true, in multiple stories unfolding and being told, in our effort to see and engage each other as fully human, always literate, and always becoming.

Rachael Gabriel
October 2022

Introduction

How did you become literate? When you think about how you learned to read and write, what experiences stand out? Was it enjoying bedtime stories with a parent or sibling? Writing your name with magnetic letters on the refrigerator? Chanting letters and sounds in your kindergarten classroom? Listening to family stories and dreaming of writing your own? Practicing spelling words Monday through Thursday, so you could ace the test on Friday? It is likely that experiences like these, whether joyful or agonizing, contributed to your development as a reader and writer. Becoming literate does not happen all at once or through a fixed set of experiences; it happens over a lifetime, and our literate identities are shaped by our experiences both in and outside school. Early school experiences are particularly important in the journey to becoming literate. They are most effective when teachers work with children and families to build knowledge about how language and texts work while, at the same time, meaningfully engage them with a wide variety of texts for various purposes that are relevant to children's backgrounds and cultures.

We wrote this book to challenge the media-driven messages about how children learn to read, which often promote a narrow view of early literacy instruction. While recent media has called attention to one important element needed for effective reading—the ability to decode print—we are concerned that as attention is funneled toward policies and programs that focus heavily on word reading, other necessary dimensions of literacy education are being ignored. We resist any form of literacy education that is reduced to a single view and instead present a framework that includes four interrelated dimensions that, when attended to by well-informed educators, contributes to literacy development. Our framework for active literacy learning (ALL) is intended for educators seeking evidence-based practices that reflect a range of knowledge. The four dimensions revolve around *meaning making*, which is central to all literacy learning:

- learning the codes
- reading and writing with purpose
- building confidence and competence
- engaging critically with texts

Educators, in partnership with families, create inclusive learning environments by building knowledge across these dimensions. When instructional decisions are informed by a wide range of knowledge, instruction supports learners as they use literacy to thrive. At a time when the politics surrounding literacy education are driving toward narrow and mandated content that serves some students well, but leaves others behind,

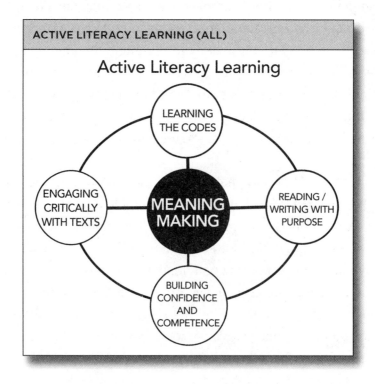

we invite readers to join us in thinking through the complexities of becoming literate and embracing multiple views and perspectives to meet the needs of all learners.

We write for educators who teach and nurture children who are learning to be literate. These are children who are competent with literacy skills and confident about themselves as literacy learners and users. These are children who learn to engage with literacies as tools for learning and communicating, and who will be successful in school and in life. Throughout this book, we recognize the value of open and trusting relationships between educators and families. Our approach is not to share a recipe, or a specific method of teaching. Instead, we intend for readers to consider knowledge within and across the dimensions of our framework and why the framework is necessary.

We know literacy learning is a cognitive ability that is also social and contextual. Thus, approaches to literacy teaching must take into consideration cognitive growth in tandem with the diverse interests, experiences, and motivations that influence learning. For these reasons, we feel strongly that a variety of methods are essential to meet the diverse needs of children in classrooms. We will not argue for or against teaching that uses terms such as *structured* or *balanced literacy*. In fact, to the extent possible, we will avoid these terms altogether, as they have become divisive in the discussion about how to teach children to read. Our aim is not to add to the dissension nor to persuade readers to adopt a particular method of teaching or instructional program. Rather, we intend to provide information; to draw upon research from multiple fields; and to share the best of what we know about teaching young children to read, write, and become engaged, competent, and confident literate citizens. We are unabashedly on the side of every child who is striving to become literate.

THE POLITICS OF EARLY LITERACY INSTRUCTION

The most effective ways to teach children to read and write, particularly when they first enter school, have been debated for many years. The debate is political. In the media, and subsequently in the public sphere, it has been dubbed the "reading wars." The war metaphor implies that there is a right and wrong way to teach all children to read. It positions people to choose a side and to be loyal to their choice, rejecting all experiences that do not uphold the perceived beliefs and practices of the side they have chosen. The early battles in the war were between phonetic and whole word approaches to teaching children to read. With the introduction of whole language philosophy in the 1980s, many conflated whole language with whole word approaches, mischaracterizing whole language as a technique for identifying words that minimized decoding in favor of guessing based on pictures and context. As time passed, labels changed. The current battle is between structured literacy (an approach that privileges systematic phonological awareness and phonics instruction in early reading) and balanced literacy (an approach that, as its name suggests, balances instruction across components of reading: phonemic awareness, phonics, fluency, vocabulary, and comprehension; and instructional structures: read-aloud, shared reading, guided reading, and independent reading). Although some labels have changed, the conflict persists, and periodically, the media develop new metaphors and thrust them back into public discourse. Importantly, these metaphors reinforce narrow political views as simple solutions to complex problems, distracting researchers and educators from crossing boundaries to embrace complex solutions.

Political Use of Metaphor

The intentional use of metaphor to disseminate messages to the public is a common strategy used by the media to normalize certain ways of thinking and talking about political issues. As humans, we make sense of the world through metaphor. Metaphorical thinking allows us to understand complex concepts, ideas, and processes in terms of other, more common, knowledge. Metaphor guides our thinking at a subconscious level. We encounter metaphors regularly in our daily lives and use metaphorical language to communicate. For example, we routinely think of time, an abstract concept, in terms of money. We use phrases like, "that was time well *spent*," and "I've *invested* too much time in this project." Although we know that time is not actually the same as money, phrases like these activate the conceptual metaphor "time is money," making it possible to understand time as something that can be spent, invested, or wasted, like money. Because metaphors guide thinking at a subconscious level, they can be used strategically to influence public discourse surrounding political issues like reading education.

The reading wars metaphor is activated with expressions like, "Balanced literacy is increasingly *coming under attack*" (Gewertz, 2020, para. 6), "Leaders of the science-based reading movement . . . have *a new target in their sites*" (Gewertz, 2020, para. 30), "the panel published a 449-page report that was a *crushing blow* to the whole language movement" (Hanford, 2017, para. 38). Such language, found frequently in media stories about reading education, perpetuates an either/or discourse around reading education, hindering civil dialogue, and obstructing the use of knowledge grounded in a wide range of research across various fields of study (MacPhee et al., 2021).

Although literacy scholars and researchers have acknowledged that the war metaphor is unproductive, and even harmful, for the field of literacy education, it continues to be prevalent in media accounts of early reading instruction and in public discourse (Kim, 2008). In the most recent iteration of the reading wars, the term *science* is being used in the media as a weapon to discredit educators and promote a narrow view of reading and reading instruction; it is a view that focuses almost exclusively on decoding in the early years of schooling. These media narratives promise that such a focus will solve the reading crisis and address issues of equity in education. Although we know that attention to phonics in the early grades is necessary, it is neither sufficient, nor appropriate, as the sole focus for early literacy curriculum. Instead, early curriculum must address the full spectrum of what it means for learners to develop as literate individuals.

Metaphors and Educational Norms

The media assertion that "all brains are the same" suggests learning to read can be conveyed as a single story. The argument implies that if all brains process letters and sounds in the same way, then all children should learn in the same way——from the same systematic and explicit curriculum. With this thinking, a single story becomes the norm. One consequence is that learning to read becomes understood through a medical metaphor. Children who fall outside the norm are diagnosed with a deficiency, viewed as unwell, and prescribed a treatment. This medical metaphor guides education policy and many school practices. It reinforces an understanding of (dis)ability solely as an internal characteristic of a child rather than as related to conditions in the environment.

A second consequence of singular thinking about reading development positions children from diverse cultural and linguistic backgrounds at the margins. Indeed, such marginalization remains visible as intractable "gaps" in standardized test scores, as well as out-of-balance referrals for some groups of students into special education and as the recipients of school disciplinary actions (Ladson-Billings, 2006; Muhammad et al., 2021). These institutionalized inequities, which often go unnoticed, socialize educators to view difference as deficit. As a result, attention in the field remains on fixing or curing children who do not fit the norm as opposed to restructuring the learning environment to respond to the needs of all children. Even more problematic is that within this metaphor all stories that don't fit the norm are erased.

In this book, we privilege a knowledge base that is inclusive of multiple stories and that positions those closest to learners, families and teachers, as experts and partners in making informed decisions about literacy teaching and learning in specific sociopolitical contexts. Thus, we hope to leave the reading wars metaphor and the single story of how children learn to read behind and move ahead to consider stories that reflect the multidimensionality of literacy learning.

MORE THAN A SINGLE STORY

We view literacy as more than a single story. There is a compelling TED Talk found online in which Chimamanda Ngoza Adiche (TED, 2009), a Nigerian author, describes her encounters with issues of social and racial identity across cultures as "more than a single story." That is, depending on the context in which she finds herself, she is viewed and views herself in the world differently. As a child growing up in Nigeria, Adiche, a Black woman, learned to read and write with British literature as her models. She realized later in life that all the characters in books she read were white with light hair and looked nothing like her. She was unconsciously defaulting to a description of beauty accepted in the literature she encountered. Later, living in America, she was also astonished at the attention given to her racial identity. She was surprised by the separation of people by race in America that did not exist in her homeland. Her message, that what we often accept as reality is actually constructed socially, aligns with our message about what it means to learn to read and write. Correspondingly, learning to read and write are complex processes that encompass multiple cognitive, social, and contextual dimensions that can be found in our ALL framework.

OUR STORIES

As educators and scholars who recognize that literacy development is not a single story, and that it is intricately entangled with identity, purpose, and power, we began this writing adventure by reflecting on our own stories of literacy learning. We acknowledge that our stories are broadly told. Although they lack specific detail, they demonstrate clearly that literacy development is not a single story, and they provide a lens through which we will consider the dimensions of ALL.

Pat Paugh

I come from a family of readers. Much of my preschool years were spent with a parent choosing books weekly from the town library. The pleasure of choosing my allotted number of picture books each week was not unlike a trip to the candy store. As I grew older, it was a thrill to walk myself into town and pick out chapter books and eventually adult literature; fiction, historical nonfiction, and biographies were my genres of choice. Those trips on my own were integral to my growing independence. When I was sent to a new high school outside of my town, without the friends I had grown up with, I sat in the library buried in books, too shy to reach out to the tightly bonded groups of girls in my class who had been lifelong friends. Books provided shelter as, at my own pace, I eventually worked out my social life. As a teacher and teacher educator, I realize the role that book choice and joy of reading play in the development of a reader's identity—not only as a student but as a person.

My younger brother, also from our family of readers, was not always a happy match with school. Bursting with curiosity and energy, he often balked at sitting still during a long school day. He was at his happiest roaming around in the woods with his friend, looking for discarded treasures found in abandoned bottle dumps, or visiting, and eventually working at, the local nature museum caring for various rescued wildlife. In retrospect, he did not fit the norms of compliance that often equate with school success. On top of this, he was not a good speller. Elementary school teachers tried to mold him, sending him to special education support classes where he was tasked with walking on balance beams, the intervention du jour for a child who did not pay attention. In high school, this same noncompliant student took the New York State Regents exam, earning a college scholarship. Looking back, I wonder with all the interventions intended to mold him as a school-conforming learner, known now as *ableism*, did anyone notice that all along he was a proficient if not an advanced reader—albeit a terrible speller.

College took him a long time, with several stops along the way. Yet he became a paramedic, ultimately serving at the highest levels of the New York City Emergency Medical Services and saving many lives during the aftermath of 9/11. He also authored a column for the *Journal of Emergency Medical Services*, welcoming a spelling editor at all times. His experience informed my own development as a teacher, the need to understand and be responsive to the talents and ways of knowing of the children in our care. A love of science engendered from his experiences with nature, a caring soul, and perseverance in fielding paramedic training resulted in a career as a medical professional in a major city, contributing to the social good. My brother taught me that the structures of schooling are not always the gateways to successful learning, and when we highlight *conformity* in learning over *diversity* in learning opportunities, we risk erroneously sending a message to many highly intelligent students who don't "fit" the system that they are not competent learners.

As a college student, I found a place for myself as a psychology major preparing to teach elementary school. My favorite professor was an adjunct who also was a reading specialist. His experience working with high school students who were struggling with literacy shaped his teaching. Similar to messages communicated in today's media, he felt strongly that early development of the foundational skills, especially word decoding, was key to reading success. He made sure that his teacher candidates had a full range of knowledge about the factors important in early reading development. When we learned about phonics, we were expected to read and process seminal studies about decoding available in the early 1980s. He also made sure that we understood and reviewed a range of commercial reading curricula so that we would distinguish the different types of phonics instruction—synthetic and analytic. I remember pouring over Jean Chall's (1967) *Learning to Read: The Great Debate.* Our professor also sent us to the research to look at factors beyond phonics instruction. It was at that time I was introduced to linguist William Labov, whose work demonstrated the danger of assumptions made about children's language competency due to invisible social and cultural norms. I am forever thankful that my professor did not stick to a single story but urged us as novice teachers to pay attention to multiple stories as we educated ourselves deeply to be responsive to the students we taught. I am also thankful for the expectation that our curriculum review included in-depth reading. This sent a message that we were preparing to be professionals, not technicians at the mercy of commercial curricula.

In my own teaching as a professor of literacy education, I think back to my transition into early elementary teaching and my subsequent 20 years as a K–12 teacher, 14 of them in first-grade classrooms. As someone who was educated in my college program about the importance of phonics, I eagerly jumped into my role bringing a well-developed, systematic understanding about teaching sound and letter patterns and word decoding. I was proud to say I could teach a "mean short e." However, I also remember a pivotal experience, looking at my students and realizing that this instruction was not connected to any purpose for *why* we were learning all of this. At this point, I began to investigate the role of meaning-focused instruction. I found high-quality children's books, a few of which were beginning to include characters of color and girls who were *not* princesses. I ordered sets of these with my weekly book order points. I added book discussions to my reading program, drawing on resources such as Junior Great Books discussion protocols. I educated myself about the integral connection between reading and writing through conferences on writing workshops. All the while, I never felt the need to "switch off" the explicit phonics instruction, but I did see the value in expanding my early-literacy instruction to invite meaning making and active use of literacy as equally beneficial in shaping my young learners' literacy experiences.

Deborah MacPhee

I grew up in a small city in the northeastern United States where I walked to and from elementary school each day with a group of neighborhood friends. I do not specifically recall when or how I learned to read and write, but I have vivid memories from my early years of schooling of plaid phonics workbooks, weekly spelling tests, and round-robin reading groups. I was quite astute at completing worksheets and memorizing spelling words. My stellar performance readings of paragraphs or pages in basal readers kept me in the "high" reading group throughout those years, even though I never experienced reading a whole story because instead of paying attention to what my peers read, I practiced the section I would need to read in front of my teacher and peers. I have few memories of writing in the early grades beyond learning to write my name, writing my spelling words ten times each, and copying or crafting sentences that included my spelling words.

I am from a working-class background. My parents valued education and expected me to bring home good grades and conform to the norms of schooling. My early success in learning the skills of reading and writing meant that I was considered by my teachers, peers, and parents to be a successful student. I was even tested for the gifted and talented program. I did not qualify. As I continued through school, I read what my teachers required and comprehended well enough to respond with some success to the multiple-choice questions that seemed always to follow assigned reading. I completed writing assignments. My writing was accurate and simple. I did not take risks and was rewarded for this with fewer red marks on my papers than were earned by my peers, solidifying my identity as a good student.

Although from early in my schooling I possessed the skills to become a proficient and voracious reader and writer, I rarely, if ever, chose to read or write on my own. Reading and writing were school activities. They were the things I had to do to be successful in school. So, I did them, and based on school standards, I was successful. I assimilated to the norms of schooling at the time. I was, for the most part, well-behaved. I completed my work with a high level of accuracy, and my teachers liked me. However, I did not see literacy as relevant to me outside of school, and since my grades were good (not exceptional), and my literate identity was intact, it never occurred to me that I might be missing something. I was truly shocked when I was placed in a remedial writing course in my freshman year of college, where I majored in elementary education. I took the remedial writing course and moved through my undergraduate program with relative ease. I spent my first five years of teaching in first grade where I taught reading in much the same way as I learned to read; heavy on skills, light on intellectual engagement. I earned a master's degree during this time, completing readings and assignments as I always had.

Still feeling like there was more to learn, I began taking courses toward a doctoral degree. This is where I was introduced to the socio-psycholinguistic view of reading (Goodman, 1967). Completely new to me at the time, the shift from thinking about reading as an accumulation of language-based skills to a process of problem-solving and meaning making helped me understand myself as a reader and changed the way I engaged with texts. Finally, reading and writing became purposeful and meaningful to me. I felt an urgency to exercise the intellectual freedom I felt. I became a voracious reader of both academic texts and literature. I threw myself into my doctoral studies, and as an educator I became a strong advocate of whole language practices.

In reflecting on my experiences with literacy learning and teaching, I have come to understand the harmful effects of being swept up in the reading wars. I learned to read and write and began my teaching career firmly grounded in a phonics/skills-first model of literacy learning. Although I do not regret time spent learning the skills of literacy, I do have regrets about what I missed as a result of my constrained early literacy experiences. Many years passed before I realized the value of engaging with texts, authors, and ideas. As an educator, when I finally came to this realization, I pivoted from one extreme stance to another (the other), rather than acknowledging the value of experiences across a spectrum of knowledge and instructional methods.

With some distance, and a great deal of reading, thinking, and talking with colleagues from a range of perspectives about early literacy learning, I approach this book not from an extreme position but rather from a more moderate position informed by a wide range of research and many years of working with early literacy learners and educators. Over those years, I have learned that literacy learning exists at the center of a complex network of interrelated dimensions, and that as educators, we must attend to a range of knowledge and value children's diverse experiences to effectively meet their needs in inclusive classroom communities.

Four Literacy Themes Revealed

Reflecting on our own stories reinforced what we have learned elsewhere, through our education and experiences as learners, teachers, and scholars with long-standing interest in literacy learning. Our stories are just a small sample of what learning to read means in the context of school and everyday life and across time. Both stories demonstrate what Deborah noted above: learning to read is more than a single story— instead it is learning that exists at the center of a complex network of interrelated dimensions. Our stories alone point to the different trajectories that influenced our development. They also offer some themes to consider as we engage with what counts as the evidence-based knowledge about literacy development.

One theme that stands out is simply *the benefits of choice*. When choosing and evaluating texts for interest, relevance, or purpose, readers develop independence and autonomy. That is, they think for themselves and think across purposes and perspectives. When the focus of reading is limited to good grades or, in current times, scores on state-mandated tests, the focus on reading and writing for one's own reasons may be lost. Instead, a learner seeks to please a parent or teacher who is the one in charge. Students who are in charge of their own learning through choosing, evaluating, and critiquing literacy texts not only learn how to read and write, but they also learn why it is important to do so. They develop the personal power to use literacy for purposes relevant to their own lives. They develop a relationship with books. As Deborah noted, when she realized reading was a meaningful activity, she moved from thinking about reading as merely an accumulation of skills to seeing it as the means for intellectual work.

Neither of us has ever negated the importance of skills in our learning or teaching. However, we realized that there are powerful effects when, in addition to developing skills, readers also have simultaneous experiences choosing books that interest them and engaging in formal and informal conversations about the ideas in the texts. There is some dominant thinking about literacy learning that positions "skills first," also termed *learning to read*, followed by instruction in making meaning, known as *reading to learn*.

When teaching first grade, a middle school colleague, who ascribed to the learn to read/read to learn model, told Pat, "Spend time on the skills when they are young, we'll teach them to understand later."

To which Pat replied, "If a student does not see literacy as a meaning-making activity when they are young, why would they suddenly be ready to think deeply about text meanings later in their school years?"

Having early opportunities to make choices is to learn to be in charge of one's literacy. This is an aspect of identity. We hope that children grow into the understanding that literacy is something they "do" and not simply a set of skills they learn to please the teacher. A healthy literacy classroom offers *both* skill development *and* opportunities for learners to see texts as purposeful and useful for their own intentions.

This leads to another related theme, *learners' development as competent, active users of literacy*. As we saw in our stories, children receive powerful messages about what it means to be literate from an array of life experiences. We anticipate that readers of this book will be educators, and possibly families, seeking to ensure that children develop strength as literate people. Of course, literacy is strength in preparation for a good job, but it is also strength to read, write, and question for the good of others and for society. We are witnessing the power of media, especially social media, to create and shape beliefs. We are also witnessing the power of those narratives to influence changes in laws that limit opportunities for health care, voting, and civil rights. So, we hope that children see their literacy as power to participate in society by questioning, rewriting, and creating informed texts of their own. As linguist James Gee (1992) reminds us, literacy is a verb, something people do. Thus, it is vital that along with developing strong literacy skills, early literacy experiences situate children as active, competent, and self-directed learners.

A third theme is the *assignment of positions to students*. Are all students positioned as competent, or are some relegated to categories of deficiency? Because both of us are white, and primarily speak, read, and write English, our experiences do not include what it means to learn literacy across more than one language. Our life and school experiences do not include racism and linguicism. Often, expectations that mirror white culture are accepted as the norm for how children learn. Ways of knowing outside of a single cultural model are often invisible in how research questions are asked, the way research is conducted, and how it considers what is "normal." For example, April Baker-Bell (2020) who researches the experiences of students who speak Black English (also known as African American English) reports that Black students continually experience societal messages that devalue how they speak. This is despite Black English being a distinct language system with a rich history and complex syntax. These students possess language and cultural backgrounds that offer a rich array of resources for learning literacy. Yet, those resources are often rendered invisible in an educational system where the goal is standardizing instruction through a single story. Consequently, rich language resources are often erased from curriculum that prioritizes basic skills in pursuit of "Standard English" as a norm. This is not to negate the need to make sure children are learning what they need, but to consider as in our stories, that there are multiple dimensions to that process.

Related to all the above is *the role of schooling in a reader's development*. How learners experience school has implications for how they experience learning and themselves as learners. How schools organize teaching and learning around what is considered normal has significant impacts on instructional priorities. As Pat recollected, her brother's experience represents a story seen all too often. The systems of schooling are designed to assign a status of deficiency to children whose ways of learning don't match singular expectations for what a learner "looks like." How often do we hear talk about students as "levels" or "tiers" with limitations put on their instructional opportunities? When labels become attached to a learner, learning strengths can be rendered invisible and learning opportunities delayed. Most teachers will acknowledge that no classroom contains a group of homogeneous learners who learn at the same pace and rate. Diversity in language, culture, and ways of learning *are* the norm. Yet, schools are structured to sort students into programs of instruction, both inside and outside their classrooms. And much of professional development in schools focuses on implementation of commercial programs (often with a set scope and sequence) rather than emphasizing knowledge to adopt and adapt an instructional design suitable for their context.

TEACHERS AS PROFESSIONALS

When programs, rather than students, are central, systems in schooling continue to restrict teachers' roles to that of technicians rather than professionals. In addition, many teachers, especially in school districts with inequitable funding, are expected to teach two curricula. That is, the one they plan for across a year, and a second one, that is aimed at preparing students specifically to perform on high-stakes assessments. Prioritizing standardized assessments steals time from teachers noticing children's day-to-day learning and their being able to adapt the classroom-focused data that *they* collect to create daily instruction for access and success. Therefore, we argue that systems of schooling must support teachers with tools for inquiry-based professional learning that enables them to make knowledgeable decisions about curriculum and instruction.

Our point is that teaching is a profession. Yet, teachers across time, and of course in current times, face outside messages about how literacy should be taught. These messages too often result in real pressure for teachers to conform to narrow instructional programs and practices. As Deborah noted, she experienced pressure to shift between extreme viewpoints, rather than receiving encouragement to engage intellectually and to make decisions about responsive instruction within her teaching context. In this book, we invite readers to engage intellectually, to take a questioning stance, to consider and reconsider current knowledge about literacy development. That is, we hope you bring your own stories and join us in exploring the many dimensions involved in the complex endeavor of learning to be literate.

OVERVIEW OF THE BOOK

In **Chapter 1**, we provide background on what it means to become literate in today's world and rationale for teaching early literacy through an integrated approach that embraces multiple dimensions rather than a single story. We provide three guiding questions and encourage readers to forefront these as they read. What do we know about how people learn? What is literacy for? What is a text? We then introduce the ALL framework that includes four dimensions of knowledge relevant for educators as they explore their own understandings of literacy development. The ALL framework provides information that will be helpful in planning instruction to support all students.

In **Chapter 2**, we expand the notion of codes in literacy learning and address the benefits of code instruction as part of a responsive curriculum. We position learners as codebreakers and focus on word-level codes (phonics, orthography, morphology), text level codes (sentence and text structures), and language codes (language variations, code-switching, translanguaging). In doing so, we move away from the single story or simple solution to reading success that confuses word identification with reading.

We draw attention in **Chapter 3** to the importance of purpose in literacy teaching and learning. All reading and writing is purposeful. We contend that attention to early readers' transactions with texts is as important as explicit instruction in the codes and must be situated alongside it so that young children develop an understanding that literacy is a necessary tool for full engagement in society. In this chapter, we center intellectual engagement with texts, highlighting vocabulary development, questioning, and interactive read-alouds as supportive instructional strategies.

In **Chapter 4**, we argue for shifting the focus from messages about deficiency to messages about assets. We challenge school practices that sort children based on invisible norms which undermine their identities as competent learners. We assert that the most effective instructional practices are those that are responsive to the cultural and linguistic assets that all children bring to school. These foster both competence and confidence in children as learners. Finally, we summarize guidelines and practices that challenge all learners to meet high-expectations and at the same time recognize the expertise they bring from their lived experiences.

Young children engage with texts in meaningful and purposeful ways. Teachers scaffold meaningful engagement by regularly inviting them to think about and discuss ideas related to high-quality, relevant texts. These students begin to view literacy not simply as something they can do, but as something they can use to transform their worlds. In **Chapter 5**, we explore the benefits of teaching early learners to read, write, and think critically; to question texts and authors; compare texts; and compose texts from their own perspectives. We share strategies for selecting and pairing texts, as well as techniques for reading with and against the grain of a text.

In **Chapter 6**, we invite readers to reflect on the goals and aspirations suggested by the ALL framework. We address teaching, particularly the teaching of reading, as a political act and discuss how systems of schooling might support teachers in their endeavor to support all children in becoming fully literate. We advocate for teachers as professionals, encouraging intellectual engagement and decision-making based on knowledge from within and across the dimensions involved in active literacy learning.

learning
to be
literate

CHAPTER 1

Becoming Literate in Today's World

Learning to be literate is a complex process, and there are many factors that contribute to successful literacy development. Before choosing and implementing any program of instruction, responsible educators take time to examine how and why literacy functions in today's world. In this chapter we provide such background. We address various terms connected to literacy. We propose three important questions about literacy in the world today. Finally, we elaborate on our framework for active literacy learning (ALL), which highlights the interrelated dimensions that teachers, such as Ms. Gorman, described in the classroom vignette below, consider when designing instruction. This classroom teacher does not depend on one "method" in opposition to another, but rather is an instructional *designer*. That is, in planning instruction, she draws on the full scope of knowledge necessary for her to support young learners to develop as strong and independent, literate people.

MS. GORMAN'S THIRD-GRADE CLASSROOM

Before the official day begins at East End Elementary School, third-graders arrive to a room painted yellow, with wooden floors and large bright windows. There is still a slate blackboard on one wall, a vestige of the school's age dating back to the early 1900s. However, this is partially hidden by a large portable smartboard that is shared by several classrooms. The students in this class love the time of day before the bell sounds. This is unstructured time when their teacher, Ms. Gorman, is checking lunch tickets. Adult family members might stop to greet each other or family friends in English or in some of the languages spoken in this city neighborhood: Spanish, Polish, or Vietnamese. One parent walking her daughter to the classroom door, smiles as she meets one of her cousins handing in a permission slip.

The children are begging the teacher to let them use the class's iPad tablets. They hope to play Minecraft, an online game. However, their teacher will only give them permission to use the tablets for shared reading of some digital graphic novels or for playing math games. The teacher and some families have mixed opinions about video games. On one hand, a game like Minecraft challenges children to collaborate with others while they think and plan strategic moves—thus providing a chance for higher level reasoning. On the other hand, the themes of some games involve weapons and violence. Thus, access to online games is blocked on school devices.

After about 15 minutes, most children have arrived. Ms. Gorman signals them to the rug area near shelves with an array of books. The school is one of many in the district that does not have funding for a school-wide library, and so local city librarians lend the teacher batches of books each month. This month many of the books include fictional and informational themes about gardening and plant science. After attendance and opening greetings, they review the day ahead. First on the agenda is the reading instructional period. Next, the class will walk to a nearby vacant lot where volunteers have been keeping a vegetable garden as part of an urban farming program. The program organizers invite neighborhood residents, including school children, to help grow vegetables for a local farmer's market. The market provides fresh produce in a city neighborhood where the grocery stores are not always well stocked with affordable choices. Today, the class will learn about how to compost plant material and create soil for next spring's planting. The students will later write about what they have learned in science-themed notebooks that they keep throughout the year.

READING, WRITING, OR LITERACY: HOW DO THESE TERMS CONNECT?

The activities in Ms. Gorman's Third-Grade Classroom illustrate multiple aspects related to the literacy demands important in today's world. The children engage in skill-focused reading and writing instruction every day. At the same time, they also witness how literacy is useful in the context of their community. Through reading and writing about issues of food production in their local neighborhood, they use literacy to scaffold learning about science of plant life as well as social issues like food security. They also use literacy to develop community through time spent interacting with texts that are both digital and paper based. Language and literacy resources are important in relationships that bring together different cultures, languages, and perspectives vital to students' worlds in and out of school. Reading, writing, speaking, listening, viewing, and creating are all forms of literacy valued in this classroom.

Engaging in productive dialogue about literacy instruction requires full consideration of what it means to be literate in the 21st century. Even the use of the term *literacy* holds different meanings for many of us. What actually counts as literacy? Do we mean reading? Or writing? Or both? What about digital texts that include visuals and sound? Is that literacy? We may hear the term *literacies* as a plural, meaning that there are different literacy practices for different types of literacy, such as digital literacy, financial literacy, cultural literacy, exploration of good literature, or literacy essential to participating in STEM (science, technology, engineering, and mathematics), history, or other specific fields.

In media and general conversation about reading and writing education, there is an assumption that literacy is the ability to decode and pronounce words (reading) or encode and print words (writing), prior to the more complex task of critically engaging with texts, that is, applying thinking and reasoning to sounds, symbols, words, and phrases that make up texts. We agree, instruction in learning relationships among sounds, symbols, and structures is essential for understanding the logic of how words work. Yet a person must do a lot more than accurately decode and pronounce words to achieve the central purpose of reading, which is extracting and constructing meaning.

Reading is an active process that involves more than taking meaning from an existing text, it is *meaning making*. This involves negotiating meaning by bringing background knowledge to the text itself and engaging in a critical process of analyzing ideas to generate new knowledge (Norris & Phillips, 2002). Thus, decoding is essential but not sufficient to what is considered "reading" (Luke, 2018). In the same vein, to spell individual words and write grammatically correct sentences is essential but not sufficient for school success. We must also consider whether our students see their writing as more than strings of accurately encoded words. They must see themselves as composers who are creating meaning as authors—not simply as scribes.

As we will develop further in this chapter, reading and writing also involve making sense of texts that mix print, video, audio, and other media. For even our youngest students, access to information includes not only books with print and illustrations but also interactive texts with images and sounds that shape how meaning is made. As we saw at East End Elementary, digital platforms are embedded in our lives and the lives of our youngest learners. This reality requires us to keep our focus on teaching students how printed words "work" as being essential to what is important for effective reading, *while also* including explicit and scaffolded instruction on how to "read" and "write" (or compose) texts that may include multiple sign systems such as those mentioned above.

In schools we see the consequences of not fully defining reading and writing as practices that are interactive and related to language development. First, reading and writing are often taught as self-contained subjects separate from each other and separate from other content (e.g., science and social studies) even in the earliest grades. Unlike Ms. Gorman's classroom, there are many schools where reading and writing are not taught as related subjects. In fact, in many classrooms where high-stakes testing is the focus, writing is limited to training students to answer test prompts. When we don't stop to consider how reading and writing develop in tandem, and how they are part of language development, we miss the chance to provide mutually reinforcing learning opportunities for students.

Second, reading and writing are often taken up in schools as universal skills rather than as practices that support meaning making. Such a narrow understanding situates reading and writing as neutral processes or sets of strategies that can be learned and applied broadly for all purposes and contexts. Further, characterizing reading and writing as universal skills minimizes the need for attention to individual learners' backgrounds and purposes for engaging with texts, agency with respect to how texts can be used, and identities as learners and literate citizens. From our perspective, reading and writing are verbs: things people "do" to create and communicate meaningfully for many purposes and to engage intellectually in their communities. In this way, we define reading and writing not as sets of skills but as a set of social practices that are "conducted in a particular context, with a particular reader and text" (Serafini, 2012, p. 30).

Finally, reading and writing are often taught in ways that deny the range of linguistic resources students bring to their literacy development. In a changing world, students need to develop concepts about print in a context where they are asked to understand what language is, how it relates to literacy, and their roles and goals for being literate people. As demonstrated in the vignette, classrooms in the United States include speakers of multiple languages, including varieties of English (such as Black or African American English) and languages other than English. A teacher who considers the multiple language resources learners possess and uses them to explore "how language works" in different ways and for different contexts, values rather than erases existing linguistic knowledge. Linguistically responsive instruction in this vein looks across codes and discusses the power of different codes for different purposes.

Exploring how languages work (the concept of language) encourages learners to be *language aware*. This opens the door for them to develop expanded repertoires of language and literacy resources rather than solely assimilate to the dominant language. Losing existing language resources is a consequence of a narrowed curriculum. Conversely, expanding language resources has the potential to open new understandings about language, including language involved with becoming literate.

Educating children who are learning to be literate requires us to think broadly. Therefore, moving forward, we will use the terms *reading*, *writing*, *comprehending*, and *composing*, yet we always regard these as developing in relation to each other rather than as separate entities. We ask our readers to join us in thinking of literacy as involving all of the above and shifting away from traditional views of learners as recipients of skills and strategies as ends in themselves (what Paulo Freire terms a "banking model" where knowledge is deposited into learners' heads). Instead, we ask that readers consider learners at the center, as agents in their learning of skills and strategies needed for effective reading and writing, and as users of literacy to design their social worlds both in and out of school.

WHAT IT MEANS TO BE LITERATE IN THE 21ST CENTURY: THREE KEY IDEAS

Day-to-day teaching in most schools is a demanding role that requires us to juggle myriad responsibilities and involves a sharp focus on the present. Keeping up with the immediacy of classroom life usually leaves little room to reflect on what counts as literacy in today's world or to think ahead about preparing learners who will be ready to adapt to rapid changes over the course of their lives. For these reasons, taking time to make visible our values and goals for literacy education requires intentional mindfulness.

We offer three questions that denote areas that influence literacy education and provide a broad rationale for instructional choices. These prompts provide food for thought as we identify the reasons why we choose to work within and across multiple dimensions when creating literacy instruction. These areas are pertinent to the needs of young learners and also relevant in shaping their capacity for future literacy learning. We situate them here as questions to guide much of what you will read in subsequent chapters: What do we know about how people learn? What is literacy for? What is a text?

What Do We Know About How People Learn?

Literacy education that responds to the complex demands of today's world challenges many traditional structures for learning embedded in our educational institutions, and even for the assumptions we hold about how people learn. As the millennium approached, a movement of researchers conducted a synthesis of research on human learning. The National Research Council (2000) report, *How People Learn* draws on research in multiple fields, such as psychology, computer science, sociology, and biology to develop deeper understandings about human learning. This report is connected to an evolving field of study known as the learning sciences. Researchers in the field of the learning sciences attempt to understand the intersection of cognitive development and social context; with important implications for curriculum design, instruction, assessments, and learning environments.

Learning scientists seek to understand how the brain works in conjunction with the context where the learning occurs. These specialists argue for instruction that looks very different from the "stand and deliver" teacher-directed practices that have dominated classrooms in the past. Instead, they emphasize the importance of deeper conceptual understanding. Scientific studies across cognitive neuroscience and developmental psychology indicate that experience and social collaboration are necessary factors for long-term concept development. For example, learners who have opportunities to develop language and literacy through a process of *use* build and connect synapses in the brain—forming neural networks for that knowledge to *transfer* and be sustained. Let's take a school-related example—vocabulary instruction.

A typical homework assignment in elementary school might be to memorize vocabulary definitions for a weekly test. From a learning sciences perspective, if the goal of classroom learning is limited to test performance—that performance may actually interfere with development of learners as active users of knowledge (Bransford, 2007). Instead, vocabulary learning can be a more useful and active process. If students are tasked with sorting vocabulary words into patterns or concept categories, they are more actively building knowledge through meaningful use. This type of activity is more likely to lead to retention or "stickiness" of the ideas in memory (Brown et al., 2014).

A learning sciences perspective also challenges traditional school practices such as studying subjects separately. Instead, units of study that are collaborative and project-based, such as the garden unit taught by Ms. Gorman, provide opportunities for teachers to explicitly teach skills as they scaffold instruction for their students to use them purposefully. To do this, teachers must become well-versed in the literacy demands required for projects. Then they are prepared to scaffold the learning so that children increasingly participate in choice and problem-solving needed for the project's design and success. The learning sciences prompt us to understand instruction as a means to develop learners' "future flexibility" or the ability to use literacy to adapt and innovate in ways that lead to changing ourselves, our environments, or both (Bransford, 2007).

Of course, humans are more than brains, which necessitates a final note about any assumptions we make about learning and the brain. Zaretta Hammond (2020) argues that we must carefully consider the learning sciences in conjunction with research on education that is culturally relevant. This means we must consider how the brain develops in conjunction with current systems in place in our educational institutions (Hammond, 2020; Compton-Lilly et al, 2020; Milner, 2020). There are embedded structures of schooling that sort and separate learners based on assumptions about innate ability or disability. Most notably, the oft-cited "achievement gap" for Black, Indigenous, and people of color (BIPOC) and English learners should force educators and families to take a critical look at unexamined assumptions about teaching that position learners as somehow deficient.

There are hidden assumptions built into the way society views intelligence and competence. The convergence of research within the learning sciences challenges fixed notions of intelligence, instead indicating that the brain is malleable and responsive to environmental experiences. This supports considering the effects of instructional designs that acknowledge learners' social, cultural, and linguistic funds of knowledge and builds on these—always with high expectations for next steps. Without examining institutions such as schools, which are structured without such consideration, so-called reforms continue to reproduce instruction that is harmful to some groups of learners (Willis, 2019). The metaphor of a "gap" itself becomes a deficit view of learners who do not fit a particular view of learning success. There are exciting conversations in the educational world that urge us to look not only at cognitive or brain development but to also understand the intricate relationships between brain development and the experiences of the learner in the world.

In thinking about how people learn, we must additionally consider how this knowledge helps us make decisions about literacy instruction. Today's students will benefit if educators take up the challenge to expand our knowledge beyond what has traditionally counted as literacy instruction. Only well-informed educators can design high-expectations curricula (Dudley-Marling & Michaels, 2012) that cultivate strong literacy identities for our youngest learners. We owe it to students to use the best knowledge available in designing instruction, which may also require challenging existing practices that have historically limited student opportunities.

What Is Literacy For?

Ms. Gorman's students are not only learning skills for reading and writing; through their community gardening work they are also using literacy as a tool to engage with issues around food production. For instance, children learn to consult books to answer questions about growing plants. One favorite book in the classroom collection is called *What the World Eats* (D'Aluisio & Menzel, 2008) in which students explore their own local food knowledge, comparing it with information about food resources around the world. Their teacher also uses the seed packets from the garden as texts for teaching vocabulary and different forms of writing such as procedures or explanations. They capture notes in their journals and learn writing genres that helps them to create instructions and information for family and community (see Paugh & Moran, 2013).

Ms. Gorman's classroom is an example of the explicit teaching of literacy skills along with a critical and local awareness about how language and literacy relate to participation in students' worlds. Becoming literate prepares learners to actively engage with economic, environmental, and social issues. Children need to use their literacy as a tool for multiple purposes now and in the future. As learners begin their journeys toward literacy, it is important to consider the skills that will aid their development and allow them to simultaneously understand reasons for why they need to learn these skills. We ask our readers to examine some of the thinking behind the reading standards and programs that are found in classrooms and to consider how, or whether, these fit with such larger purposes.

The world has shifted from a manufacturing economy to a knowledge economy. This shift illuminates tensions with how literacy has been traditionally taught. Many jobs of the past are no longer relevant, and evolving technologies and products require new and different skills. In the United States, a major initiative in updating literacy education resulted in the widely adopted Common Core State Standards (CCSS) for English Language Arts and Mathematics (National Governors Association, 2010). As of this writing 41 out of 50 states have adopted these standards and their related assessments. This national standards movement has a stated focus on "College and Career Readiness." Supported by foundations funded by private business and technology industries, such as General Electric and the Bill & Melinda Gates Foundation, the main intention of instruction based on CCSS is to prepare grades K–12 learners for the types of jobs available in these new times. A focus of CCSS, and others such as the Next Generation Science Standards (NGSS), is to move learners beyond only procedural learning of foundational or basic skills, toward higher levels of reasoning and application of those skills. For example, engineering and technology require problem-solving and creative thinking. A related focus is for instruction to address specific literacies for different disciplines such as language important for STEM fields. Therefore, the CCSS have expanded to three different areas just for reading (reading foundations, reading literature, and reading information) as well as others for language, speaking and listening, and writing. When we attend to the multiple stories of what counts as literacy development, we must consider the relationship among these different aspects related to learning to read and how reading relates to the other language arts.

While adopting a curriculum that accesses jobs and rebuilds the workforce is essential for rethinking employment in these new times, there are other essential elements that are not included when literacy education is solely aimed at economic goals. Our classroom vignette hints at the diversity of language, ethnicity, and cultural backgrounds that students bring to most classrooms. A classroom context such as this frames the larger need for social literacy goals. Social literacy practices provide tools to understand and communicate with others who bring different perspectives from their community and across the world. These practices are needed for issues of citizenship, that is, participating with others in society both locally and globally. Calls for social and critical literacy instruction can intersect with the goal of improving literacy for economic access but push further to challenge current thinking about equity and social justice. For example, a 2014 United Nations Education, Scientific, & Cultural Organization (UNESCO) report on global citizenship education for the 21st century argues for education to place increased "emphasis on the importance of values, attitudes, and skills that promote mutual respect and peaceful coexistence . . . beyond cognitive knowledge and skills . . . to help resolve the existing and emerging global challenges menacing our planet" (Global Education Monitoring Team, 2014, p. 9). In the United States, prompted by the deluge of online information and misinformation shaping our current political discourse, there are related calls for literacy that will enable citizens to fully participate for civic and democratic interests (Coles, 2000; Milner, 2002).

As schools have focused through the CCSS on the goals of educating for changes in the economy, and relatedly on disciplines that are directly connected to rising industries such as health care or technology, other subject areas that promote the simultaneous development of social, emotional, and cultural awareness have taken a back seat (Greene, 2021). Subjects like philosophy, literature study, social studies/

history, and especially the arts have been deemphasized in curriculum that looks to vocational training and the hard sciences. The latter being the programs of study that are more likely in the short term to result in lucrative employment and growth of the economy. Jobs and economic growth are important goals. Yet, teachers and community leaders (and even business leaders in high-tech fields) are increasingly noting that instructional programs do not sufficiently balance sciences and vocational training with courses in the liberal arts. Thus, liberal arts courses take a back seat in school and college programs. As the liberal arts support learners to imagine new ideas and recreate new relationships with others and our physical world, their elimination poses serious consequences for participation in not only the workplace but in society.

What Is a Text?

If we stop and see what people are reading and writing today, we may notice that we are doing more than just reading and writing print. Over the course of a day or week, we also view and listen as we engage in a range of literacy-related events. Like the children at East End Elementary, we may use a computer tablet to access information or entertain ourselves with a game. We may also consider and share opinions on social media by developing a message that requires a combination of photos and print. We may skim the news on our iPhones while simultaneously checking our weather apps and sending text messages. If we have family, friends, or colleagues far away we may be able to speak with them directly through Facetime. In fact, as authors, we have been writing this book between distant states, requiring us to use document sharing as a collaborative writing tool and Zoom as a digital meeting space. These are just a few examples of how living in today's world requires literacy that enables people to navigate information in formats that are digital, visual, and aural/oral, and often a hybrid of some or all of these.

Around the time we celebrated the millennial, educators began to anticipate how literacy was changing. An international meeting of scholars, known as the New London Group (1996), issued a reconceptualized model for literacy education: *A Pedagogy of Multiliteracies*. The group argued that traditional definitions of literacy were no longer valid, and they proposed expanding the view of what counts as literacy. The texts we encounter are often composed of multiple formats, or modes known as multimodal ensembles (Jewitt & Kress, 2010). That is, a text might consist of images and/or sound along with print. It might contain hyperlinks to other texts such as a website. While the familiar printed texts remain part of our lives, it is necessary to consider "reading" as more than only the decoding of print. Also, texts we encounter cannot always be read in a linear fashion from beginning to end. This changes how we think about what an effective reader or writer "does" with a text. Consequently, classroom literacy education for contemporary times must prepare learners to not only read, but to view, respond, and produce multimodal and digital texts from the earliest years. Building on the New London Group, literacy educator Frank Serafini (2012) proposes that we think about readers as "viewers, navigators and designers" because the variety of texts today require that we make decisions about how to process the combinations of different modes we encounter. He points out that technology is changing and will continue to change what counts as literacy now and in the future. Thus, instruction cannot remain in a time where written texts are the only source of information.

While certain relationships with written texts, such as reading novels, will not change, other texts require that learners be prepared to work across multiple sign systems. One key message that has come across in recent media about early reading instruction is that children must understand how to decode print using phonics. This is valid. However, accompanying this message have been sweeping statements that until students' master decoding, they should not have access to texts with images, such as picture books, to read independently. The concern is that if students use pictures as part of reading, they will never learn to decode print. As former teachers in early education classrooms, we know it is possible to notice and provide explicit instruction to students who are avoiding, or not attending fully to the print, while also teaching them how to use illustrations to construct meaning.

Removing or covering illustrations or other visual images in the texts young children read is one example of an extreme practice that distorts the very nature of the reading process—*to make meaning*. Furthermore, it limits opportunities to explicitly teach children how to make sense of multimodal texts, which are becoming increasingly prominent in today's world. It is imperative that alongside learning to decode, readers begin to understand the relationships between print and other modes. Hence, a more flexible view toward what is important for early literacy instruction is warranted.

As recently as 2021, the National Council of Teachers of English (NCTE) offered the position that to "imagine the future and beyond . . . literacy and language arts education must include the study of media texts, genres, platforms, and institutions" (Aleo, 2020). In these times, to design effective literacy instruction, we must consider an expanded definition of texts based on what 21st-century readers and writers are expected to comprehend and compose, and to adjust to a broader range of ways in which information is created, disseminated, and received.

A DIET FOR HEALTHY LITERACY DEVELOPMENT IS MORE THAN JUST TEACHING SKILLS

Many of the messages surrounding questions about effective reading instruction are not only delivered as a single story, but at times are presented as a set of many separate single stories. What we mean is that these messages fit a model where skills are taught before meaning making, and reading is modeled as a set of skills that are frequently taught as separate entities. The action of reducing reading to its component parts can be problematic, particularly if it causes educators to neglect the larger picture of what literacy is for and what it means to learn to read and write. This phenomenon related to breaking instruction down into bits or parts can be mirrored in a similar argument about the effect of vitamins in maintaining a healthy body. While we often take a range of different vitamins to boost specific nutritional requirements, we know there is great variation in different vitamins for different bodies or even different vitamins for all bodies. In fact, there is evidence that too high a dose of some vitamins can have deleterious effects on our health (Price, 2015).

Just as there is no evidence that an array of different vitamins would ever replace the role of healthy food, we need to consider our understanding of skills, or components, important to literacy development. Like vitamins, there are skills involved in effectively reading a text. And using this same metaphor, a teacher, like a doctor, needs to know each component—skill or vitamin—and how they function together. For example, today's media highlights brain research findings that phonological awareness (the ability to notice speech sounds in language) is a key factor in the effective decoding of printed texts (Compton-Lilly et al., 2020). There are children who for many reasons do not develop this awareness naturally and need specific instruction to attend to these sounds, as well as how they are represented in print. Systematic teaching of phonics (e.g., the sound/symbol relationships in alphabetic texts) is put forward as the tool for providing these children with the knowledge they need to be effective readers.

There are further suggestions that providing a specific "structured" program of phonics to all children might then be a preventative measure to ensure that phonological processing skills are attained. Yet the single focus on "prescribing" phonics as a solution that guarantees reading success, just as prescribing vitamin C tablets for all people, is not enough. International literacy researcher Alan Luke (2018) addresses the problem with single solutions by highlighting the distinctions of *necessity* and *sufficiency*. Possessing the phonological and phonemic connections for decoding words is necessary but insufficient if the instruction does not include other key components important to teaching children to be strong and fully functional users of literacy. Therefore, educators must know the full range of factors important for effective reading and writing and how these factors work together. We must also know our students and the background knowledge, values, and resources they bring to the process of becoming literate.

The framework for ALL depicts four broad dimensions of knowledge integral for learning and teaching at all phases of literacy development and the dynamic relationships that exist between and among these. It is our sincere hope that this framework provides educators and families who wish to engage with their children's schools a wide lens through which to consider how children become competent and confident literacy learners and users.

A FRAMEWORK FOR ACTIVE LITERACY LEARNING (ALL)

The framework for ALL depicts four dimensions of knowledge integral for learning and teaching at all phases of literacy development. We contend that each of these dimensions and how they interrelate must be fully considered in the pursuit to educate children who are learning to be literate. By situating children as meaning makers at the center of the framework, we hope to move beyond a single story. These four dimensions of knowledge related to effective early literacy education are:

- learning the codes,
- reading and writing with purpose,
- building confidence and competence, and
- engaging critically with texts.

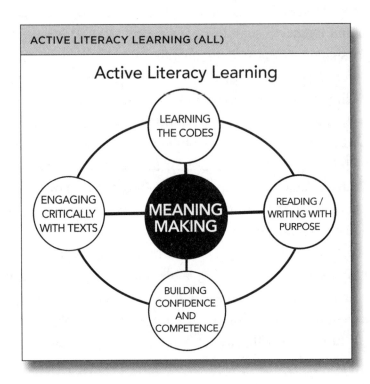

Importantly, these dimensions are related and meant to inform literacy instructional programs where the central goal is preparing readers and writers for *meaning making*, the point of being literate!

Why We Developed This Framework

Our interest in what counts as effective early literacy instruction coincides with messages being communicated through media and organizations such as the International Dyslexia Association and/or National Council for Teacher Quality that are reaching schools, our state departments of education, and some states where legislatures are enacting laws that govern literacy instruction in individual classrooms. These media messages have sparked considerable attention to early reading education, and this is a good thing. On the other hand, how messages are presented reproduces long-standing oppositional arguments about how reading should be taught and reinforces a view that there is a single story, or simple solution, that will result in all students becoming successful readers by the end of third grade. The ALL framework is intended to provide information necessary for teaching the codes that underpin accurate and efficient word reading. It is also intended to provide knowledge about other important considerations that may be getting lost in the current conversation.

Additionally, our reasons for developing this framework coincide with social movements such as Black Lives Matter, and relatedly, recent political events requiring critical reading and viewing of news that spans a range of ideologies. Becoming literate involves learning to read words and also seeing oneself as an agent in brokering meanings communicated through those words. To this end, we must position our youngest learners to think deeply about ideas and language in high-quality texts at the same time as they learn the skills for working out the sounds and symbol systems of language. As former first-grade teachers, we know that young students notice the world around them. They are definitely capable and interested in asking important questions and talking about big ideas. Instructional programs for all young children need to include these opportunities.

Lately, we have been following social media conversations among teachers who wish to create the best possible literacy programs for their young students. Increasingly, we notice teachers who have a strong desire to learn more about word decoding (areas such as phonological and phonemic awareness, phonics, morphology) are also asking about other dimensions of early reading education. For example, we notice teachers inquiring about the importance of early comprehension through interactive read-alouds of quality children's literature. We notice questions about how to handle visual information in books and media. This convinces us of the importance of attending to an expanded view of what is important for literacy development, and subsequently, how different instructional goals and practices can strengthen early literacy programs.

How This Framework Joins the Conversation on Effective Early Literacy Instruction

In the framework for ALL, we seek to highlight knowledge across different related dimensions important to early literacy. This is knowledge that teachers and families should consider as they create instruction for children. This is knowledge that comprises important factors for cognitive learning along with the social, cultural, physical, experiential, historical, developmental, and linguistic resources that enable learners to successfully engage with texts. Our framework, and our teaching, is inspired by the work of researchers and literacy educators who share our goals, draw on each other, and from whose thinking we also draw upon in our framework.

For example, the four resources model (Freebody and Luke, 1990) was developed as a response to the familiar debate about the explicit teaching of phonics or more holistic "whole language" models for literacy education. The model offers four resources that are relevant to all literacy learners at all times, rather than a hierarchical structure that limits exposure to some resources at particular points in development. This model has been revisited and incorporated into teacher education as well as recent successful school reforms in Canada's Ontario province (see Luke 2018; Shirley, 2021). The model offers four components important for instruction within a unified reading program: coding competence (ability to decode a text), semantic competence (the ability to participate in making meaning of text), pragmatic competence (the ability to use a text within a context or for a purpose), and critical competence (the ability to question and analyze text). Alan Luke, recently reflecting on the use of this model, noted that it is not a developmental model but a model where all four components are meant to be incorporated from the first three years of literacy instruction onward.

Zaretta Hammond (2015) presents brain research in conjunction with culturally responsive instruction. In her book, *Culturally Responsive Teaching and the Brain*, she argues that instruction emerging from neurological studies demonstrates the need to engage learners early in complex cognitive work that explicitly teaches skills and simultaneously responds to learners' social, emotional, and cultural identity formation. In our own experience in schools, we've seen instruction that prioritizes skills as a single story, believing that skills must come first in order for complex learning to occur later. However, along with Hammond, we've seen this thinking delay intellectual development for students who may need intensive and specialized skills instruction yet are quite capable of higher level thinking and problem-solving. Similar to the four resources model, Hammond promotes instruction that honors multiple stories by advocating for teaching across cognitive and social learning goals in the primary grades.

Another unifying instructional model that we draw upon is historically responsive literacy (HRL). In this model, Dr. Gholdy Muhammad (2020) combines critical theory, sociocultural theory, and cognitive theory in a practical instructional framework to foster both personal and academic development. Based on her study of African American literacy societies that emerged following the U.S. Civil War, Muhammad's framework challenges the single story offered by traditional skills-only instruction. In addition to (and not a replacement for) instruction aligned with standards and skills, Muhammad's model offers teachers space for teaching and assessing students' identity development, intellectualism, criticality, and joy. In essence, Muhammad's model is based in humanizing practices. She writes that if teaching and measuring skills are the only measures of achievement, rich and equitable literacy development cannot advance as a humanizing endeavor.

In addition to the models mentioned above, we are drawn to a metaphor for integrated literacy instruction presented by Dr. Rachael Gabriel. She asks teachers (and all of us) to envision literacy development in line with plant or tree development (Gabriel, 2021). A plant grows below and above the soil. We can consider skills development (especially that relating to word decoding) as the roots or foundations of a plant absorbing minerals and nutrients from the soil. At the same time, a plant sprouts branches and leaves that absorb sunlight and air. These above-ground nutrients also nourish the plant. The above-ground growth is what Gabriel envisions as language exposure and meaningful comprehension of text. Envisioning a plant growing in this way, helps us think about the relationship between skill instruction and development of literacy as a practice (learned through purposeful use). Over time, both dimensions flourish if well cared for. As a gardener, author Pat understands the benefits and consequences on her seedlings when there is too much or too little water. She also checks frequently to see when her plants need fertilizer or compost. In the same way, as educators, we must assess learners to ensure that both skills and meaningful use of text are growing together.

An Asset-Based, Evidence-Based, and Responsive Framework

Along with our colleagues mentioned above, we draw on knowledge gained from our own years of teaching early literacy as well as a wealth of evidence from research that convincingly argues for more than a single story in defining early literacy instruction. With this framework, we seek to provide a knowledge map for readers to reflect on guiding beliefs and practices related to early literacy learning and to invite new learning about areas that might not have been visible. We have placed meaning making at the center of the frame and surrounded it with dimensions important to efficient and effective literacy development. Our framework for ALL considers the ultimate goal for literacy, using the words of linguist Michael Halliday, as essentially "learning how to mean" (1975). Although we present these dimensions thematically, we emphasize that they are all essential and interrelated. You may notice that each dimension in the framework changes position as we feature it in different chapters. This is because the framework is not meant to be static but always moving to indicate the importance of the variety of knowledge needed to build programs of instruction for young children. Basically, our framework embraces countless stories to reflect the many beautiful and unique children in classrooms. It widens the lens on early literacy learning so that you can be well-informed about asset-based, evidence-based, and responsive teaching for the children in your care.

CHAPTER 2

Learning the Codes

When literacy educators engage in conversations about teaching children to read in alphabetic language systems such as English, we often refer to "breaking the code." Breaking the code typically means that students need to understand relationships between graphemes, or the symbols of written language, and phonemes, the sounds of oral language that are represented by those graphemes. Young children then use this knowledge to identify, segment, and blend letters and their related sounds to unlock unknown words. In this chapter, our goal is to examine

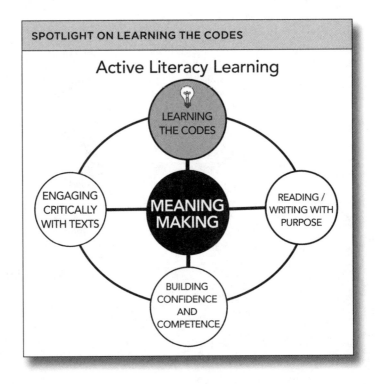

SPOTLIGHT ON LEARNING THE CODES

Active Literacy Learning

LEARNING THE CODES

ENGAGING CRITICALLY WITH TEXTS

MEANING MAKING

READING / WRITING WITH PURPOSE

BUILDING CONFIDENCE AND COMPETENCE

how sound/symbol relationships—also known as phonics—are integral to successfully extracting and constructing meanings from text. We also consider an expanded notion of *code* to include syntax and text structure as language codes and use this notion of learning the codes to explore how printed texts work at other levels of language. The syntax, or grammar, of language, as well as the different organizational structures authors use to interpret and convey meaning also constitute codes that contribute to meaningful comprehension of text.

Next, we share the ways in which Mr. Hall, a first-grade teacher, is learning about how language works at the word, sentence, and organizational levels. He is building on his own professional learning to design reading instruction through which he explicitly teaches his first-graders to be aware of these codes or systems as they build their own tools for unpacking texts.

MR. HALL'S FIRST-GRADE CLASSROOM: PART ONE

In mid-November, Mr. Hall, a first-grade teacher, reviews student data from his district-mandated foundational reading assessment. He notices that after the first nine weeks of school his first-graders demonstrate a range of knowledge in phonological awareness (identifying patterns of sounds in and across words) and phonics (recognizing how sounds match to letter patterns and using these patterns to decode unknown words) that are helping them progress as readers. Mr. Hall reflects that recent professional development at his school focused on these and helped him better understand English as an alphabetic system. That is, he is using his understanding of how sounds (phonemes) and symbols (graphemes) match to assess how well his students are beginning to identify phonetic patterns and to use them strategically to figure out unknown words. Because English is the target language of instruction at his school, Mr. Hall can use this knowledge to better interpret assessment data compiled from the district testing conducted three times a year; he can also utilize it to construct more frequent informal checks on student progress from week to week. In this way he can compare information from both sources and differentiate instruction as needed by creating small teaching groups during his literacy instructional block.

To promote practice and confidence in word recognition, Mr. Hall provides decodable books. His first-graders are so proud to show him and each other their growing fluency as they read increasingly complex words and sentences in these books. At the same time, he realizes that decodables are only one important type of text for building strong readers. He also makes sure to introduce his students to different sorts of texts that have more complex language and ideas. For this purpose, he incorporates interactive whole-class read-alouds and guides students to recognize how texts build ideas. Each week, students plead to "help" him at story time, where Mr. Hall reads and rereads narratives, and students act out character roles. Through conversations while reading, they also "help" him analyze text structures, such as the sequence of story events. In this way he is modeling and scaffolding their understanding of how stories are constructed.

Mr. Hall knows that some of his students speak primary languages that are not English, so he has made time to learn more about the languages they speak and to investigate whether these students are already literate in those languages. He encourages all his students to be "language aware." For example, with his learners who speak Spanish as their home language, he guides them in comparing sounds in the Spanish alphabet with those in English, valuing their language and using it as a resource for instruction. Mr. Hall grew up speaking African American English. While he informally shares the different choices he makes as a speaker with his students, he hopes to strengthen his knowledge about using home-language resources productively in his teaching.

Through his teaching, Mr. Hall pays explicit attention to structural aspects of language, including but also beyond the word level. He knows that many early readers and writers bring knowledge of more than one language to their literacy learning. In this chapter, we address the importance of examining relationships across languages to support all readers. The endgame is to position readers as agents, or code breakers, who always use their knowledge about how texts work in service to the more central purpose of all literate activity: meaning making.

A SIMPLE OR COMPLETE VIEW OF READING?

The simple view of reading (SVR) model (Gough & Tunmer, 1986) has played an important role in the field of reading education, contributing greatly to our understanding of decoding and its relation to language in the reading process. The model, most commonly depicted as a mathematical equation (Decoding × Language comprehension = Reading comprehension) is used to explain reading comprehension as the product of decoding and language comprehension. In this model, decoding and language comprehension are believed to occur independently and sequentially (Duke & Cartwright, 2021). Developed in 1986, its simplicity is appealing to educators and curriculum developers, and its influence on reading instruction is evident in schools and classrooms.

Recently, research conducted through the Reading for Understanding (RfU) initiative has validated the importance of developing students' word-reading skills in the early grades. This research has also called into question the claim that decoding and language comprehension are independent components of reading comprehension. This independence, or separation, of decoding and language comprehension has led to a narrow focus on decoding in the early grades at the expense of meaningful attention to language. Critics conclude that such a narrow focus, which is how the model has been taken up in recent media, may misrepresent the SVR and certainly "overlooks the importance of early language development as fuel for both decoding and comprehension" (Cervetti et al., 2020, p. 4). Further, they suggest that language development is best understood and taught as "an interconnected set of skills" that are "mutually reinforcing . . . that is, many language skills are invoked in the process of reading, and thus, the coordination of these skills during reading may create a system of linked development" (Cervetti et al., 2020, p. 6).

Other researchers recognize the value of the SVR model but promote a more complete view of reading (Francis et al., 2018; Snow, 2018). For example, Francis and colleagues (2018) posit that although the basic claim of the SVR has held strong, it is only a partial representation of the knowledge and interactions that result in reading comprehension. From their perspective, comprehension is the end product of complex interactions between a reader, a text, and an activity, and "the quality of this product depends on the skills that the reader brings to the task, the demands that the text places on the reader, and the challenge posed by the specific activity in which the reader is engaged" (Francis et al., 2018, p. 274).

The SVR model was developed through research that focused only on the skills of the reader, or what Francis et al. refer to as the component skills framework (CSF). Reading research, they argue, is characterized by two additional research threads: the features of text and linguistic discourse and the development of reading. They refer to these threads as the text and discourse framework (TDF) and the developmental framework (DevF). They argue that these threads typically run parallel to each other and that each body of research, although valuable in its own right, is limited in its explanation of reading comprehension. Their response was to develop a new model, which they call the complete view of reading, that accounts for the variation within readers and across texts. Despite its name, they and others acknowledge its incompleteness, in that it does not represent "variation among readers in the ability to perform the tasks of comprehension needed for local and global citizenship, for human understanding, and for moral analysis" (Snow, 2018, p. 315).

We celebrate the SVR model for what it has contributed to our understanding of reading and reading instruction. At the same time, we recognize that by itself, the model does not address the full range of knowledge necessary to effectively support early literacy development. In both research and media accounts, more attention has been devoted to the decoding side of the SVR equation than to the language comprehension side. The practical result of this unbalanced attention has been the development of assessments and instructional programs that focus on word reading and related skills, thereby minimizing the importance of oral language development in early reading. One consequence of this overemphasis on word-level instruction in the early grades is that reading becomes defined as *decoding*—and learning to decode print becomes an end, rather than a means, to making meaning. For this reason, as we noted above, it is important to expand our understanding of codes beyond sound/symbol relationships to include language patterns at the syntax and text structure levels and to position our knowledge of codes alongside our knowledge of texts and students.

When English, as an alphabetic language, is the target language, understanding the relationships between sounds and symbols is critically important to becoming a competent and confident user of texts. Literacy researchers have invested much time and energy investigating how young children learn to decode print and exploring when and how it is optimal for educators to teach them to do so. The focus is mainly on how print decoding facilitates automatic word recognition. However, there is substantial evidence that instructional attention must also be dedicated to sentence level and text level structures that convey meaning and purpose.

When reading and writing instruction privileges word-level decoding and encoding, we become concerned about what is left out. Are we unwittingly conveying the message to children that reading is only about pronouncing words, or that writing is only about correct spelling? In the next section, we focus on word-level codes; in subsequent sections, we discuss sentence level and text level structures and how explicit teaching of those structures can also be considered part of the process of unpacking the systems within a language such as English. Thus, we expand the idea of *codes* to include the role of language systems and structures in how texts are created, and in how readers and writers actively use language in order "to mean" (Halliday, 1975).

WORD-LEVEL CODES

First, the basics. English is an alphabetic language. That is, it is made up of distinct speech sounds that can be represented by letters and letter patterns. The individual sounds within words in alphabetic systems are called *phonemes*. A phoneme is the smallest unit of speech that distinguishes one word from another. Words are made up of various combinations of phonemes, which in written language map onto various combinations of letters in an alphabet (*graphemes*). Included in learning the codes is learning to unpack these combinations within words in order to decode novel words, an instructional method known as *phonics*. Explicit instruction in learning phonics is currently at the center of many questions about how best to teach early readers, and historically, at the center of the many controversies in the field of reading education. Therefore, we will begin our discussion of language codes with information about phonological processing, including a discussion of various questions related to phonics instruction—which is the teaching and learning of letter/sound relationships within the graphophonic system.

Phonological Processing, Orthographic Mapping, and Self-Teaching

Phonology is a branch of linguistics concerned with how sounds are systematically organized within particular languages. Phonological processing is the use of sounds to process spoken or written language. There are three components in phonological processing.

- *Phonological awareness* is an awareness of the sound structure of a language and the ability to hear and manipulate individual sounds. Children who are phonemically aware can segment words into individual sounds and blend individual sounds into words.
- *Phonological working memory* refers to how phoneme information is temporarily stored in short-term memory, so it is readily available to complete phonological awareness tasks.

  • *Phonological retrieval* is the ability to recall phonemes associated with specific graphemes. (Wagner & Torgesen, 1987)

Phonological processing is crucial to reading development because it facilitates the orthographic mapping process, allowing readers to recognize words automatically without the need for phonological recoding, or letter-by-letter decoding (Compton-Lilly et al., 2020).

Additionally, there is a large body of brain research establishing the importance of phonological processing in early reading development (Dehaene, 2009; Ehri, 2014). Neuroscientists have associated phonological analysis and recoding with several areas of the brain. As young children gain knowledge of grapheme/phoneme relationships and practice decoding novel words, they activate these areas and strengthen their neural network for reading.

Phonological processing also facilitates *orthographic mapping*, which is the process for how words are permanently stored in memory, and it explains how children learn to read by sight and spell from memory (Ehri, 2014). According to Ehri, orthographic mapping, "involves the formation of letter-sound connections to bond the spellings, pronunciations, and meanings of specific words in memory" (p. 5). Studies have linked phonological processing and whole-word recognition to age and experience differences; beginning readers rely more on phonology-based reading, and more-skilled readers process text at the orthographic, or whole-word, level (Share, 2011; Ehri, 2014).

Orthographic mapping is not a skill that can be directly taught. Rather, it is enabled by phonemic awareness and phonics knowledge, and it is facilitated by word-level instruction that combines grapheme/phoneme relationships, pronunciations, and meanings of novel words. When the orthographic mapping process is activated, children begin to learn more about how words work through reading. This is known as the *self-teaching hypothesis* (Share, 1995). According to the self-teaching hypothesis, children's ability to decode novel words is the primary way by which they acquire orthographic knowledge. Although decoding skill does not guarantee orthographic learning will take place, the self-teaching hypothesis assumes that every successful decoding of a new

TABLE 2.1

SELECTED PHONICS CONCEPTS AND RELATED SPELLING RULES

Phonics concepts	Examples	Related spelling patterns and rules
Single consonants	b, c, f, g, l, m, p, r, s, t, v, w	Hard and soft c and g
Short vowels	a, e, i, o, u	Syllable type: closed
		Closed syllable patterns: CVC (pet, sip, lob) CCVC (brag, clog, spin)
Digraphs	ch, sh, th, wh	
Initial blends	cl, fl, gl, br, tr, sp, st	
Final blends	ld, lf, lk, lp, nd, nt, mp, st, ft	Spelling pattern CVCC (band, gift, jump)
Three-consonant blends	scr, str, spl	
Digraph + consonant	shr, thr	
Long vowels	a, e, i, o, u	Syllable type: open (go, be)
		Long vowel patterns: CVCe (gave, rake, code) CVVC or Vowel teams (mail, dream, boat)
R-controlled vowels	er, ir, ur, ar, or	
Diphthongs	oi, oy, ou, ow	

word provides an opportunity to learn word-specific orthographic information that facilitates the automatic word recognition needed for skilled reading. Because phonological processing facilitates automatic word recognition and more-skillful reading, it is important for early readers to understand how sound and symbol systems work in an alphabetic language such as English.

Phonics Instruction

Phonics is a method for teaching children to decode and encode words by correlating sounds with letters, or groups of letters, in an alphabetic writing system. Research has shown that systematic phonics instruction benefits children who are learning to read (National Reading Panel [NRP], 2000). Although questions remain about what type of phonics instruction is best and how much is needed, there is strong evidence that phonics knowledge and phonological processing facilitate orthographic mapping—the process by which readers retain words—so that the sight of a word activates its pronunciation and meaning in memory. Systematic phonics instruction follows a general developmental sequence for introducing phonics concepts and spelling rules. Additionally, it incorporates decoding and encoding practice through activities such as blending, segmenting, and dictation, as well as in more-authentic reading and writing contexts. Table 2.1 presents selected phonics concepts and related spelling rules.

There are essentially two types of phonics instruction: synthetic and analytic.

- *Synthetic phonics* instruction involves teaching children letter/ sound correspondences and how to blend individual sounds into words. For example, if "c" represents /k/, "a" represents /æ/, and "t" represents /t/, then "c-a-t" can be blended to make /cat/.
- With an *analytic* approach, the focus is on combining larger sound chunks, onsets and rimes, or word families (-at, -ip, -ump, etc.), and using known words to figure out unknown words. For example, if a student knows the word *cat*, then they can use their knowledge of the -at family to figure out words like *sat*, *flat*, and *splat*.

Although you may find that proponents of systematic phonics instruction favor one type of instruction over the other, the experimental studies reviewed by the National Reading Panel (2000) showed no statistically significant difference between the two.

TABLE 2.2

PHONICS AND WORD ANALYSIS SKILLS PROGRESSION FROM THE CCSS

Grade level	Foundational skills indicators
Kindergarten	Demonstrate basic knowledge of one-to-one letter–sound correspondences by producing the primary sound or many of the most frequent sounds for each consonant
	Associate the long and short sounds with the common spellings (graphemes) for the five major vowels
	Read common high-frequency words by sight (e.g., the, of, to, you, she, my, is, are, do, does)
	Distinguish between similarly spelled words by identifying the sounds of the letters that differ
Grade 1	Know the spelling–sound correspondences for common consonant digraphs
	Decode regularly spelled one-syllable words
	Know final -e and common vowel-team conventions for representing long vowel sounds
	Use knowledge that every syllable must have a vowel sound to determine the number of syllables in a printed word
	Decode two-syllable words following basic patterns by breaking the words into syllables
	Read words with inflectional endings
	Recognize and read grade-appropriate irregularly spelled words

Grade 2	Distinguish long and short vowels when reading regularly spelled one-syllable words
	Know spelling–sound correspondences for additional common vowel teams
	Decode regularly spelled two-syllable words with long vowels
	Decode words with common prefixes and suffixes
	Identify words with inconsistent but common spelling–sound correspondences
	Recognize and read grade-appropriate irregularly spelled words
Grade 3	Identify and know the meaning of the most common prefixes and derivational suffixes
	Decode words with common Latin suffixes
	Decode multisyllable words
	Read grade-appropriate irregularly spelled words

Ultimately, the purpose of phonics instruction is to enhance students' understanding of letter/sound patterns in the English writing system, so they can create and unlock meanings of increasingly more complex texts over time. It is a means to an end, not an end in itself. Table 2.2 shows how the Common Core State Standards (CCSS) have conceptualized phonics as a foundational skill in Grades K–3 instruction. This can serve as a guideline for teachers who, with a deep understanding of the phonetic system, can provide instruction to ensure that students become proficient word solvers.

As children gain and use knowledge of letters and sounds, they develop what has been called a *set for variability*. This is a reader's ability to flexibly approach the pronunciation of unknown words (Zipke, 2016), allowing them to produce accurate pronunciations from partially decoded words by changing one or more of the sound associations within words (Venezky, 1999). The concept is important because the English writing system is considered to have a deep orthography, meaning that there is not a one-to-one correspondence between sounds (phonemes) and the letters (graphemes) that represent them. This deep orthography can make reading and writing in English more challenging than in other languages that have shallow orthographies (e.g., Arabic, Latin, Spanish, Italian).

Although the success of readers using set for variability is dependent on their receptive vocabularies, studies have found that aptitude predicts the reading of irregular and regular words (Steacy et al., 2019; Tunmer & Chapman, 2012). There is growing evidence that this lexical flexibility can be directly taught (Dyson et al., 2017; Savage et al., 2018; Zipke, 2016).

Deborah, who works in a university literacy center with children who experience difficulty learning to read, supports students' flexible use of sounds to decode words. She does this by prompting students who decode and mispronounce words with language like, "Does that sound like a word you know?" and "What sound(s) can you change to make it sound like a word you know?" These prompts remind students that they can, and should, use what they know about letter/sound associations flexibly when decoding words in texts.

Teachers can observe when students begin to do this independently. For example, recently, Deborah was supporting Aiden, a fourth grader who had been diagnosed with dyslexia, as he read an article about the recent authorization of the Pfizer COVID-19 vaccine for children between the ages of 5 and 11. In the sentence, "It spreads more easily than earlier versions of the virus and in some cases can make people more sick," Aiden initially read the word "spreads" with a long /e/ vowel sound. This made sense because Aiden had learned that the sound associated with "ea" is the long /e/ sound. But he recognized that his pronunciation of "spreads" was not an accurate oral representation of the word. He immediately (and independently) changed the vowel sound to produce the correct pronunciation. At the end of the paragraph, Deborah praised Aiden's flexible use of knowledge to self-correct during reading and explained that the "ea" letter combination sometimes represents a short /e/ sound. More importantly, Deborah recognized that Aiden's ability to independently use set for variability is an indication that he is at a point in his development where he may benefit from more time engaged in reading connected texts and less time building phonics knowledge through systematic phonics instruction.

HOW MUCH PHONICS INSTRUCTION? How much phonics instruction is enough is a question that has been considered for many years. Although research has yet to offer a clear answer, Marilyn Jaeger Adams (1990), an internationally regarded researcher known for her work in the areas of cognition and education, presents an analogy that, at least to some extent, suggests that such a response is dependent on individual learners:

> *In grappling with this problem, it may be useful to think about it analogically. Code instruction may be likened to a nutrient, a basic building block for the growing reader. Extending the analogy, we see, first, that ingestion of the proper amount of such a nutrient is critical to students' potential development. Second, we realize that its proper metabolism will not occur in the absence of a balanced diet. And third, we find that—however healthful it may seem—we must be careful not to dish up too much.*
>
> *Although the consequences of feeding a child excessive amounts of phonics may not be as obvious as with food, the metaphor keeps going. The extra phonic calories do not enhance growth. They are kept as unnecessary and burdensome tissue or quickly flushed as waste. Worse still, the child may become groggily sated before getting to the other necessary and complementary items on the menu.* (pp. 50–51)

Adams, a strong advocate of explicit phonics instruction, also draws on a vitamin metaphor when she recognizes that more word-level code instruction is not necessarily better for children and may actually disrupt literacy development for some learners. Her metaphor casts doubt on the educational soundness of marching all children through scripted phonics programs until they have mastered all phonics concepts and spelling rules. Rather, educators must be knowledgeable about relationships between sounds and symbols in English, and other languages, so they can assess students' knowledge and application of word-level codes and plan instruction that supports readers as problem solvers who monitor their reading and use their code knowledge flexibly. Mr. Hall, the first-grade teacher we met earlier, uses frequent and formative assessment to discern student progress. Below, you'll see how he adapts instruction to differentiate what they need to learn as early decoders.

MR. HALL'S CLASSROOM: PART TWO

Based on his monitoring of students' progress, Mr. Hall knows that eight of his first-graders are able to segment and blend sounds in one-syllable words. Some are just learning to do so with CVC (consonant vowel consonant) forms; others are moving on to reading words with a variety of vowel sounds. One student reads texts with multisyllabic words. On the other hand, Mr. Hall recognizes that four of his students can identify initial consonant sounds in words but need further instruction listening to and matching sounds and letters in short-vowel words before they will be ready to take the next steps in decoding. He plans to play some games and sing songs with them to reinforce listening to sounds in words and manipulating them to make new words. These phoneme games set the stage for the processes behind decoding words in print. A favorite activity for these students is the iPad center set up during the literacy time. Here iPad games provide further opportunities for play with letters and sounds. While students think of this as play, the goal is for extended exposure and further sensitivity to printed text. Sometimes, small groups or the whole class take "dance breaks" and Mr. Hall invites them to move and sing songs that also reinforce hearing sounds in oral language.

Professional learning about the role of sounds and symbols in words has strengthened Mr. Hall's confidence in adapting the phonics program purchased by his school to differentiate instruction. He wants to make sure students are introduced systematically to the patterns of letters and sounds, but he had been concerned that moving all students through a paced curriculum was unnecessary for some who had already mastered concepts about phonology and decoding. At the same time, the pacing might also leave other students behind. With his growing language knowledge, he now feels more confident in adapting the curriculum to student needs as well as adding activities and challenges that he has created.

Morphology

Morphology, or the combining of meaning units to make up words, has less of a focus than does phonology in early reading. In fact, it is often called the neglected stepchild of phonology in terms of research on early literacy instruction (Share, 2021). However, there is strong evidence that effective readers use meaning units as "building blocks" to connect printed text and meaning, and to access unknown vocabulary (Rastle, 2019). It may therefore be a helpful strategy to include as explicit instruction for learning to read.

As we learned earlier, a phoneme is the smallest unit of sound in an alphabetic word. The suffix "eme" denotes *smallest*, and we also find it in the term *morpheme*. But this time, the smallest unit is that of meaning within a word.

There are two types of morphemes or meaning units. The first are *free morphemes*, which can be thought of as single standing words that represent one meaning unit. A familiar experience we may remember from our own early literacy education is the study of "base" words. The other type of morpheme is a *bound morpheme*, which cannot stand alone. Prefixes and suffixes are examples of bound morphemes that affect the meaning of a base word or free morpheme. An example is the base word *play*, which stands alone. If the bound morpheme "re-" is added to *play* the prefix changes the meaning to an action that can happen again.

Free and bound morphemes combine to form words where the bound morpheme affects both the meaning of the free morpheme (called a *derivation*) and, at times, the grammatical structure, or part of speech (called an *inflection*), of the original free morpheme. Bound morphemes may change meanings related to time (e.g., *step* in the present tense becomes *stepped* in the past tense through the addition of the "-ed" suffix) or amount (e.g., the singular *cat* becomes *cats* with the addition of the plural "-s" suffix). A bound morpheme may also change the part of speech (e.g., *sing* is a verb, adding "-er" to create *singer* changes the word to a noun). Some other morphemic information useful to readers are contracted forms such as *cannot* combined into *can't* (see Table 2.3).

All morphemes are combined in English by rules governing the ways that affixes can and cannot be added, and the order in which they can be added. So, there are regularities for many English words that readers can build into their decoding repertoire when facing new vocabulary. However, we know that while English follows these rules, there are irregular exceptions: for example, when tense is changed within a word (e.g., *run* in the present tense becomes *ran* in the past). Those of us who have observed young English speakers notice that they first demonstrate awareness of morphemic knowledge through the use of past tense or the "-ed" form. In fact, young children often overuse this as they begin to make sense of the rules of past tense. Pat used to chuckle hearing her young students speaking to each other, "Mrs. Paugh, we *goed* fast on the playground." or "James *eated* all his lunch." It's important for parents and teachers to understand that this speech indicates sensemaking about language on the part of new learners and to recognize and encourage them as learners, while also subtly revoicing the more advanced forms such as *went* or *ate*.

Because this field is understudied in relation to phonological awareness in reading, there are different perspectives about when to include morphology in early literacy instruction. A review of the CCSS for English Language Arts indicates morphology as suggested knowledge in teaching vocabulary development as early as kindergarten. The expectation in the language standards is that learners (K–12) will increasingly use their knowledge of meaningful word chunks to construct and decon-

TABLE 2.3

MORPHOLOGY

Term	Definition	Examples
Morphology	An analytical skill involving inferences about word structure and meaning	
Morpheme	Smallest meaningful unit in an alphabetic language, combined in rule-based manner	
Free morpheme	Freestanding meaning units, sometimes referenced as a base word	*play* (stands alone)
Compound word	Two free morphemes combine to create a new word	*playground*
Bound morpheme	Meaning unit that cannot stand alone	re- (prefix added to play becomes *replay*) -ful (suffix added to play becomes *playful*)
Inflections	Morpheme influences the grammatical and/or semantic (meaning) function but does not change word class	Concept of time—morpheme -ed added to verb *plant* becomes past-tense *planted** Concept of number— plant becomes plural p*lants*
Derivations	Alters the meaning of a base and usually changes word class	*help* (noun, verb) becomes *helpless* (adjective)

*English offers morphological shifts that are not simply changes through affixes. For example, many past-tense verbs do not depend on suffixes (e.g., flew, ate, ran, spent, etc.).

struct words in text (Hickey & Lewis, 2013; Rastle, 2019). Research also suggests that morphology may be an essential strategy in reading instruction for learners of English as an additional language (L2) (Goodwin et al., 2013; Kieffer & Lesaux, 2012).

Teachers who have a solid understanding of morphological knowledge can then use this across primary and secondary literacy instruction. For example, not all morphemic structures function similarly across languages. Many languages do not use prefixes or suffixes but instead place those meaning cues inside the base words. So explicit teaching of how morphemes work in English in comparison or contrast to other languages is especially helpful to L2 English learners (Hickey & Lewis, 2013). Also, many Latin-based languages (such as Spanish, French, Italian, Portuguese, Romanian) share base words, known as *cognates,* that are both visually and meaningfully similar despite different pronunciations. Since so many U.S. students are Spanish speakers, we've chosen that language as an example. Some Spanish and English cognates share spellings (e.g., doctor/doctor); others possess similarities with spelling differences (banco/bank, dia/day). Teachers who understand how morphology works can help students through the use of cognates to transfer metalinguistic knowledge from their first language as they learn to read and compose in English.

PREPARING STUDENTS TO DECODE
TEXTS BEYOND THE WORD

When we meet preservice teachers in our classes, or speak with students' adult family members, there is generally an assumption that learning to read equates to learning to "sound out" words. There is often a corollary assumption that students implicitly absorb structural aspects of text and naturally transfer the use of these to their reading and writing. As we saw in the preceding section, decoding words is a vital piece of unlocking how language works as readers build their proficiency. Additionally, we draw on the concept of decoding to mean that learning the codes goes beyond the phoneme/grapheme associations. Children must learn to efficiently decode and encode individual words as well as unlock the language structures that support their ability to comprehend and compose complex texts. We realize that the building-blocks metaphor mentioned in relation to phonology and morphology can include not only language construction with phonetic and meaning units that make up words, but also relates to the structural aspects of words, sentences, and clauses.

WHEN STUDENTS STRUGGLE WITH COMPLEX TEXTS

As children are learning to be literate, there may come a time when they begin to experience some difficulty, particularly as the texts they read become more complex. Struggle with comprehension of increasingly dense texts often becomes visible when children reach the middle elementary grades. This struggle is known as the *fourth-grade slump* (Chall et al., 1990). In Grades 1–3, (the "learn to read" years), elementary students have historically been taught using only narrative texts with simple sentence construction. When they reach the middle elementary years (i.e., about fourth grade), they are asked to read a variety of texts in different subject areas. Not only are the words in these texts longer and more abstract but the sentences contain multiple noun groups or multiple clauses. When reading more complex narrative fiction, children meet rich description where adjectives and/or adverbs appear to create fuller imagery or emotion (e.g., The *blossom-laden* branches swayed *rhythmically* in the *light spring* breeze.) Texts designed to furnish information contain multiple clauses that provide definitions or explanations for concepts in areas such as science or history (e.g., A compressed air rocket launches when air escapes downward, pushing the rocket in the opposite direction and causing it to go forward).

At this point, when students encounter such complex texts, they may suddenly present as "struggling" readers. The need for broader and earlier attention to how texts work is reflected in recent curriculum frameworks. For example, the CCSS for the English Language Arts require an earlier instructional focus on reading different texts for different subject areas. The extension of reading standards now includes two sets of reading standards, reading literature (RL) and reading information (RI) beginning in kindergarten. Therefore, there is a need for instruction to be explicit about text structures for different purposes—and for it to be taught earlier. Maria Brisk and Margarita Zisselsberger (2010) conducted research in elementary classrooms with high numbers of emergent bilinguals. They found that explicit teaching of the forms and functions of language provided valuable scaffolds for the learners to engage with complex texts. Their conclusion supports our view that the concept of decoding extends beyond the word to the level of text: that is, that the code to be cracked lies in the structures that help readers and writers effectively access the message. We agree with Reynolds and Fisher (2021) who caution, "Although complex texts can be comprehension catalysts, increasing text complexity without increasing instructional support can be a recipe for frustration" (n.p.).

There is a field of study, known as *disciplinary literacies*, that informs this expanded view of using explicit teaching of text features in the same way we emphasize explicit codes at the word and sentence levels—as tools for meaning making. Disciplinary literacies provide two areas of linguistic information that can support professional knowledge for teaching text structures: (1) focusing on how whole texts are organized, and (2) exploring syntax or grammar within and between sentences (Fang, 2012; Gryskgo & Zygouris-Coe, 2020; Reynolds & Fisher, 2021).

Organization of the Whole Text

Depending on our purpose for reading and writing, we look to specific ways in which meaning is arranged across texts. Literacies that support making sense in a variety of disciplines require unique types of texts. The expanded set of reading standards in the CCSS reflects the need to teach readers and writers about organizational differences. As such, learning the codes must include understanding patterns in how texts are organized.

When teaching literacy for a range of the disciplines, the concept of genre for teaching the *organizational analysis of disciplinary structures* is helpful to instructors. This is a slightly different use of the word *genre* than readers may be used to. Traditionally, the notion of literary genres points to differences in narrative texts such as historical fiction and fantasy. The notion of genre that is used in relation to academic texts, however, relates to areas of study not only in the English language arts but in areas such as science or history. In a disciplinary literacy sense, genre is defined as "staged goal oriented social processes" where texts are always interactive in the context of their use (Rose, 2011, p. 209). *Genre pedagogies* focus on language characteristics of specific texts based on the context in which it is being used (the social) and its purpose (the goal). Mr. Hall sets the stage for attention to how narrative and informational genres work in a meaningful context. This is explicit teaching designed to accompany texts and activities that support engagement and transfer for independent learning.

MR. HALL'S CLASSROOM: PART THREE

Along with his focus on teaching decoding systematically and providing practice with decodable texts, Mr. Hall is also careful to include explicitly scaffolded experiences with literature that are rich in language complexity. Although most of his students are not yet able to fluently decode this language, Mr. Hall understands that talk focused on well-crafted children's literature can set the stage for students to look for structural aspects of text written for various purposes.

He points out organizational features and language characteristics as he invites students to participate in interactive read-alouds. For example, when reading narratives, his students love using puppets of different characters as the class rereads a favorite story. Or students choose events using photocopies of illustrated pages to line up in sequence as they discuss how the story plot developed. After reading, Mr. Hall also asks his students to talk about alternative endings to reinforce the ideas of resolution, theme, and critical interaction. He pays attention to nonnarrative text structures as well. For example, after a trip to the apple orchard, students analyze how language works when they create and follow a procedural text—a recipe for making apple sauce.

This concept of genre in disciplinary literacies differs from literary genres (e.g., realistic fiction, poetry, etc.). In school, learners encounter multiple text forms aligned with learning across disciplines including and beyond literature study. These include genres important to schooling where the purpose may be to entertain or teach a lesson through narratives or to deliver information or to make an argument (Fang, 2012).

NARRATIVE GENRES. Narrative texts tell a story. Organizational features we expect to encounter are characters, setting, and a plot where a series of events develops a problem—and then at a climactic point, leads to a resolution. In schools, this structure is sometimes known as a *story map* or *story grammar.* Narrative genres that are found in more-informational texts sometimes simply recount a series of events, such as is provided in a newspaper report. Either way, we see that a series of sequential events is how narratives work, and readers with experience know to read a story from beginning to end or use event progression to anticipate or predict plot development.

INFORMATIONAL GENRES. There are many types of texts that provide information. A simple informational genre is *procedure,* reflected by Mr. Hall's recipe lesson. Procedures include not only recipes but also instructions for building or for playing games. While the content and context of use differs, there are common or similar features such as materials and/or ingredients, as well as steps to follow, which make this a genre. Other informational texts can be more complex, and at times combine genre features. In school, science *reports* may contain taxonomies of facts (such as a report on mammals that categorizes facts about the topic, such as food, habitat, etc.). Additionally, a report on the results of an experiment may contain precise *descriptions* of evidence, leading to higher levels of drawing conclusions or *explanations* through reasoning—which may use features of *argumentation* (see McNeil & Krajeik, 2011).

Other than a procedure, many informational texts are not meant to be read beginning to end. At times the reader identifies what information is needed and navigates to the areas of the text where that information is located. Currently, teaching informational genres often includes lessons on identifying navigational features useful for the purpose of skimming and locating information. Some of these include captions, illustrations, bold or italic words, charts, tables, diagrams, glossary, index, or graphs (Fisher et al., 2008). At the same time, teachers who guide students to connect how meanings are organized provide scaffolds for students to track certain patterns such as: compare/contrast, problem/solution, cause/effect, chronology/sequence/temporal structure, or evidence-based descriptions leading to explanations (Fisher et al., 2008).

ARGUMENT GENRES. Young children love to argue! Literacy scholars who investigate argument have found that transferring that trait to reading and writing can and should be part of early literacy education (Brisk, 2014; Lee et al., 2013). There are two types of argumentative texts: *expositions* and *discussions*. The first, exposition, entails an author arguing for a position or cause. Examples include an argument that uses evidence to convince a parent not to smoke or a campaign to reduce waste by eliminating plastic water bottles. The second, a discussion, presents opposing points of view. The issue of whether children should be vaccinated or what age people can vote are examples of topics that have at least two sides. Arguments can take the form of responses to literature, historical debates, or as noted above, reasoning related to science or math investigations. A well-constructed argument supports questioning and reasoning in a democratic society, a critical literacy topic that we'll address in later chapters.

Genre features also can be hybrid. For example, a widely used structure in elementary science education is the claims, evidence, and reasoning process (McNeil & Krajeik, 2011). That is, following a science experiment, learners are asked to describe evidence and to use that evidence to argue or reason for a key finding. Therefore, they are using language features from more than one genre—in this case both description and explanation—for the text's purpose.

Syntax or Grammar Within and Across Sentences

To comprehend increasingly complex texts in school contexts, readers must understand how to unlock meaning using syntax or grammar. Syntax represents the way that words are organized to form larger phrases and sentences. Due to the overemphasis on word learning in the early grades, syntax is an often overlooked yet important language code related to text comprehension. While research related to syntax and word identification has produced mixed results, there is ample evidence that understanding syntax in terms of word function and order is predictive of reading comprehension at Grade 3 (Deacon & Keifer, 2018; Cartwright & Duke, 2019). In fact, *syntactic knowledge* (manipulation and reflection on words in a sentence) and *syntactic awareness* (ability to break complex sentences into manageable parts) provide readers with keys to unlocking dense, information-packed texts. Syntactic complexity may be the "single most important feature that makes texts harder to read" (Deacon & Keifer, 2018, p. 82).

Teaching grammar for the purpose of reading and writing complex texts involves more than just labeling grammatical terms in the way many of us learned in school (e.g., diagramming sentences). Instead, it involves creating *meta* awareness inside a sentence, in terms of the order of words and presence of multiple clauses, analyzing how whole texts work, and guiding students to notice language across sentences that will help them build meaning. So instead of teaching students to label words with grammatical terms, teach them how certain categories of words function to help access meaning in a text. Young students can be guided in building syntactic knowledge about how ideas link together. For example, words such as *since* or *after* can be considered prepositions, but more importantly, they are words that indicate time before a phrase such as "I've had three cookies *since* lunch." Another example are conjunctions: a grammatical term for words that connect full and embedded clauses and include words such as *and* or *so* that extend an idea, or *but* or *however* that build differences. Spotting these types of words helps students develop syntactic awareness as they learn to read and write explanations and arguments (see Table 2.4).

Building a repertoire of interrelated text-reading skills involves not only syntactic markers within the sentences but also between sentences in a whole text (see Uccelli et al., 2021). An example is the use of pronouns across a text. Many of us who teach student writers find ourselves lost in

TABLE 2.4
GRAMMATICAL (SYNTAX) STRUCTURES THAT
LINK IDEAS WITHIN COMPLEX TEXTS

Grammatical structure	Definition	Examples
1. Identify clause structures	**Independent clause:** contains only one verb, stands alone as a complete sentence	Dogs are friendly animals.
	Dependent clause: phrase that connects ideas to the main (independent) clause but cannot stand alone as a sentence	—because dogs are furry According to my friend—
	Complex clause: multiple clauses that constitute a single sentence, can be independent clauses together or multiple dependent clauses all joined to an independent clause	**Two independent clauses:** Dogs are easy to care for and they are very popular with families. **Multiple clauses joined to an independent clause:** According to the SPCA, dogs have been the most frequent choices for pet adoptions due to their friendly nature.
2. Identify how clauses are connected to build ideas within a sentence	**Connectors:** often prepositions that indicate specific meanings (circumstances) **Common circumstances:** time, location, causation, reasoning, or contingency	**Time:** since (Since they moved, the house has been empty.) **Location:** under (The water fountain is under the stairway.) **Reasoning:** so (The birds are singing so spring must be around the corner.) **Causation:** because (The ice melts because it is warm.) **Contingency:** despite (We won the game despite the odds.)

Grammatical structure	Definition	Examples
3. Track pronoun references across sentences in a paragraph	**Anaphoric reference:** references to something or someone mentioned earlier in the text	The sun shines through my window. It makes the whole room nice and warm. Cargo ships are lined up in the harbor. These ships are filled with toys for the holidays.

the pronouns. That is, students often write as they speak when the subject of their talk is "in the room." But when writing for distant audiences, it is necessary to identify a person, place, or thing and then use language to ensure that pronouns such as *it, he, she,* or *they* are clearly connected as the text develops. This type of pronoun use is known as *anaphoric reference.* As texts become more complex, the opening phrases (what functional linguists call a *theme*) can reference an earlier idea. So, in a report on cargo ships, an initial statement might begin with "Cargo ships are lined up in the harbor." A subsequent sentence may reference all of this information by opening with, "*These ships* are filled with toys for the holidays." This type of cross-text reference helps an author build ideas through a text.

As the fourth-grade slump phenomenon demonstrates, school-based texts become more complex around the middle elementary grades. As literacy educators, we need to address questions about how to prepare children for reading a range of complex texts earlier. As Cartwright & Duke (2019) state in their DRIVE (deploying reading in varied environments) model of reading, syntax is key to reading comprehension, and it is amenable to instruction—that is, it may develop naturally in speech, but it may require supportive instruction in transfer to reading and writing print. Deacon & Keifer (2018) note that children who are beginning to connect their spoken words to print are typically speaking in sentences with three to five words. As they begin reading print, they can be challenged within their learning zone by guided practice with sentences that may be seven to eight words in length.

Talk centered around comparing and contrasting syntax is a fun and helpful means to value language differences for students, and is especially important for those who are multilingual or just learning English. Varieties of languages differ syntactically. As teachers, we may notice emergent bilinguals making sense of syntax by drawing on different language systems. An elementary student, literate in Mandarin, may not use plurals when writing in English. Teachers who understand that the student is bringing a range of resources to her writing can use a discussion about syntax to draw on and recognize those resources as strengths. Talking about the differences between two languages sheds light on how both work.

TEACHING THE CODES AND STRUCTURES AS ASSET-BASED PRACTICES

Keeping language codes and structures visible in the classroom positions students as language experts. One of our favorite sources for assessing student learning frames levels of proficiency within a "Can Do Philosophy" (WIDA, 2020, p. 11). The WIDA framework asks teachers to remember—as they assess students' speaking, reading, and writing proficiencies—that students always bring knowledge and learning resources to the task of language learning. Teachers taking this view work to build on what students know and can do. Theirs are classrooms where the *meta* is integral to teaching and learning.

Metalinguistic, metacognitive, and metacultural knowledge keeps the focus on what is being learned and the strengths students bring to their learning across these areas—rather than only focusing on what students cannot yet do. In this way, using what students know about language becomes the starting point for any continued literacy teaching. Positioning students as experts, and then developing curriculum based on high expectations that will advance them to their next steps, requires teachers to know both the content and the students. This knowledge then equips educators to make pedagogical choices matched to students' learning.

To be clear, learning differences are not dismissed but are looked at as design opportunities for focused instruction. In contrast, many interventions in schools consider students who struggle as deficient and in need of "fixing"—resulting in children becoming positioned as incompetent learners. Zaretta Hammond (2015), citing brain research, argues that such positioning negatively affects the cortisol in the brain, resulting in the inability to learn with confidence. Thus, all the skills instruction in the world may be negated if the learner lacks a sense of competence in their ability as a learner.

CONCLUSION

In this chapter we have proposed an expanded view of codes and how to use them to access meaning in printed text. That is, we've focused on knowledge about the structures of written language at the word level, the sentence level, and the discourse or whole-text level and considered the relationships between these. In our vignette, Mr. Hill demonstrates how he uses professional knowledge from the phonological domain to ensure that he is teaching the phonics skills that will help his first-graders decode and encode printed texts. He also provides the meta instruction by naming organizational features of text as he and his students create a recipe for applesauce. In his daily instruction, he asks his students to compare words and sentences across different languages to create a sense of reflection on language that values language in many forms. Teachers like Mr. Hill continue to seek out knowledge about language codes to provide explicit instruction to their students.

CHAPTER 3

Reading and Writing With Purpose

When readers and writers engage in literacy, they do so for a purpose. There are clear benefits to instruction focusing on specific elements of literacy, such as codes or structures to build learners' capacities. At the same time, it is essential to continually convey to young children that the ultimate goal of literacy is *making sense.* Thus, it is essential for readers and writers to always recognize their reasons for using or developing texts. Guiding this thinking is the concept of readers and writers as *text users* who remain mindful of the reasons why texts are purposeful for the social context in which they are being used (Freebody & Luke, 1990).

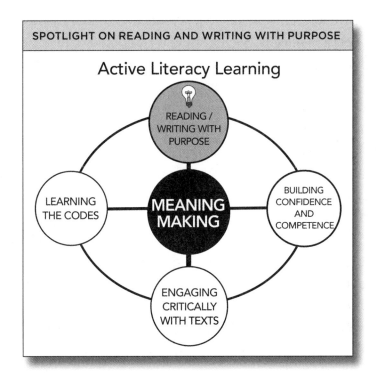

SPOTLIGHT ON READING AND WRITING WITH PURPOSE

Active Literacy Learning

READING / WRITING WITH PURPOSE

LEARNING THE CODES

MEANING MAKING

BUILDING CONFIDENCE AND COMPETENCE

ENGAGING CRITICALLY WITH TEXTS

A helpful metaphor is comparing a reader to a driver. In their DRIVE (deploying reading in varied environments) model of reading, Cartwright and Duke (2019) compare a reader determining the reason for reading with a purposeful driver who maps out a "driving destination." A driver maps out different routes depending on factors of where, when, and how they want to reach their intended destination. To emphasize purpose in literacy learning, Cartwright and Duke suggest that readers ask the question "reading what for what [purpose]?" (p. 10), suggesting to teachers and children that different purposes require a different "constellation of reading behaviors" (p. 10). Their suggestion is supported by research indicating that reading is more than a universal skill that can be applied to all texts, and that a reader's purpose affects the reading process (Zhang & Duke, 2008).

PURPOSEFUL TRANSACTIONS

Effective readers engage with texts in ways that achieve a purpose, or set of goals, for the situation in which the texts are being read or composed. Teachers support such active learning when they plan instruction that is responsive to their students' backgrounds and interests and position them as decision-makers. Such instruction embodies Louise Rosenblatt's theory that making sense is a *transaction* between the reader, the author, and the text itself. In her conception, "every reading act is an event, or a transaction, involving a particular reader and a particular pattern of signs, a text, and occurring at a particular time in a particular context" (Rosenblatt, 2018, p. 455). This notion regards each use of text as a unique event to which actors bring specific background knowledge, cultural ways of knowing, and intentions for its use in particular contexts. Importantly, transactional theory helps us avoid the trap of teaching skills as ends in themselves. Instead, skills are tools that learners transfer for their own use. According to Rosenblatt, reading a text starts with some expectation or purpose, and then skills are involved as the reader engages in a *system of choices* aimed at realizing their purpose. Readers and writers engage with the language of texts in ways where "language development involves a constant process of meaning making" (Gibbons, 2015, p. 9).

Classroom environments that develop readers as active decision-makers keep purpose at the forefront of all teaching. To do so, teachers of even the youngest learners believe that children need to be active in the transaction between readers, authors, and texts. This includes developing what we think of as a literate mindset in which learners become oriented to the multiple dimensions involved in literacy acquisition and use. This includes their own role as text users. Transacting with texts requires readers to engage in hard mental work that stretches their "intellectual muscles" in ways that result in long-term transfer of skills that stick with the learner (Hammond, 2020). High expectations for skills development can only be effective if accompanied by awareness that the learners themselves are the ultimate arbiters of how they will use these skills (and texts) for their own purposes. Below we share how a second-grade teacher, Ms. Wu, creates a literacy environment where students transact purposefully with texts with a clear purpose in mind.

MS. WU'S SECOND-GRADE CLASSROOM: PART ONE

Ms. Wu greets her second-graders each morning, welcoming them into the classroom to begin the day. As part of her routine, she and her students engage in what might seem a surprising conversation. Kendra exclaims, "Good morning, Ms. Wu. My news today is that I have a paper straw in my lunch bag. I asked Dad to buy some because they are biodegradable."

"Wow, Kendra," replies Ms. Wu, "We'll have to take a photo of your straw at snack time and post it in our *Environmental News* for this week."

The class has been reading nonfiction books on the theme of preserving a healthy environment. They've recently read *A Planet Full of Plastic,* authored and illustrated by Neal Layton. *A Planet Full of Plastic* is an informational picture book. Layton helps children access information on environmental stewardship through his use of age-appropriate examples, graphics, and fonts, such as a page with everyday trash in a setting similar to a park close to their school. While he presents a familiar scene, he also introduces sophisticated, Tier 3 vocabulary, such as *biodegradable* and *microplastics* and connects these to kid-friendly explanations. Layton's book discusses actions kids can take to prevent pollution.

Ms. Wu and her students have created a chart with three recommended actions: *Reduce* the use of plastic, *Reuse* durable plastics, and *Recycle* plastics. Later in the day, Ms. Wu will project the chart on the smartboard and the class will consider the photo of Kendra's straw and what action it represents. Jay asks Ms. Wu to photograph his reusable water bottle with a built-in straw as another example for the chart. During these discussions children relish using words in their talk that they have noticed and learned from Layton's book. They are also excited to add these two examples to a newsletter sent home to families each week.

Teachers who take up a transactional perspective rethink dominant ideas about what counts as effective literacy instruction. For example, one commonly held belief among educators and the public is that young children must master phonics and decoding before they can engage with higher level texts. This widely accepted learn to read/read to learn model conflicts with the transactional view of literacy as it directs our youngest learners away from intellectual pursuits to exclusively focus on code learning.

LIMITATIONS OF THE LEARN TO READ/ READ TO LEARN MODEL

As many teachers and families seek to understand effective literacy instruction, they often do so with an unexamined belief that literacy develops through a narrow linear pace—such as, Point A leads directly to Point B. A generally accepted guideline in the field is that children must first "learn to read" (Point A) before they can "read to learn" (Point B). This idea, which is only partially accurate, holds that foundational skills (such as the ability to decode words) must be taught and mastered before instruction focuses on gaining meaning from text. Learn to read—then read to learn is often used to reinforce the single story that early literacy instruction must focus exclusively on mastery of foundational skills prior to Grade 3. This belief leads to the delay of higher level thinking and reasoning about text until later grades. The danger in this linear view is that skills-only instruction creates a mindset in students that limits their goals for learning to read. That is, learners' initial experiences affirm the goal of reading as learning a set of skills rather than engaging in an active meaning making process. This mindset is difficult to change later (Hruby, 2020).

The belief that skills should be taught before instruction that focuses on reading for meaning remains prevalent because surface-level skills are easier to measure discretely. Dickinson et al. (2010) provide a helpful explanation for this belief in their distinction between constrained and unconstrained skills within the reading process. Constrained skills are finite. These include alphabetic awareness, concepts of print, and phonological awareness. These are skills that are readily visible and relatively easy to measure with early reading assessments that count which phonemes a learner recognizes, or whether the learner is able to identify sounds and letters, and/or whether a learner is using this phonetic knowledge to decode words. A frequent misconception when the learn to read/read to learn model is applied to instruction is that constrained skills are the gateway to the unconstrained skills needed for comprehending texts.

Unconstrained skills are comprehension-related abilities that are not always as easy to separate out, identify, and measure. Unconstrained skills include vocabulary, background knowledge, or inferential language skills. These develop throughout life and are not identical for all learners. They are introduced through interactions with texts using talk and other forms of participation and, therefore, are not as amenable to discrete assessments. Many literacy researchers argue that early literacy is the time to embrace, not delay, a focus on meaningful and purposeful use of texts alongside mastery of foundational skills. Effective instruction must simultaneously support foundational skills (learning to read) and higher level thinking and reasoning with texts (reading to learn) (Allen & MacNamara, 2020; Lennox, 2013).

DEEP COMPREHENSION

Conceptual knowledge gained from texts is related to the depth at which the texts are processed. Thus, gaining meaning entails *deep comprehension.* A quotation from the most recent edition of the *Handbook on Reading Research* challenges us to further interrogate what it means to deeply comprehend a text. Deep comprehension is more than simply absorbing a static message contained in a text but instead is an active decision-making process: "Children and youth . . . do not only need to learn to read for meaning but also need to learn how to seek, sort, and evaluate the information they read" (Moje et al., 2020, p. 4).

Research on the development of text comprehension from pre-K through 12 finds that effective or deep comprehension happens through interactions where a reader engages at multiple levels of processing. Kintsch (2018) provides a helpful guide known as the construction-integration model. According to Kintsch's model, deep comprehension stems from

surface level: recognizing the words and sentences in the text,

text-base level: activating related schema or concepts found in the text, and

situation level: creating coherence by integrating background knowledge and experiences into the text to connect with the specific situation in which the text is used.

A reader is central in navigating across these levels, not always in a linear way, but most effectively for their purposes in the situation at hand. In one research study (van den Broek et al., 2001), readers were asked to read an identical text but were given different purposes for reading:

one purpose was entertainment, another was fact finding. Interestingly, the researchers found that readers engaged in different reading strategies for each purpose despite the text being the same. Ms. Wu, featured in the earlier vignette, intentionally chooses a range of texts to encourage her students' development of the concepts around environmental stewardship.

MS. WU'S CLASSROOM: PART TWO

Ms. Wu chooses read-alouds from different text types and explicitly guides students through thinking-aloud as they read. *A Planet Full of Plastic* is a text by an author whose purpose is to provide information, so noticing factual information and how information can be presented in categories is part of the conversation before, during, and after reading. The following day, she chooses a new read-aloud with a similar theme, but one that presents different opportunities for her students to think more deeply about environmental stewardship on a global level. This time she will guide her class through a nonfiction narrative, *One Plastic Bag: Isatou Ceesay and the Recycling Women of the Gambia* by Miranda Paul (author) and Elizabeth Zunon (illustrator). This illustrated picture book is a true story about Isatou Ceesay, a woman in West Africa who noticed the pollution caused by discarded plastic bags accumulating in her community. Ceesay began a movement by creating purses from the plastic material. This true story is a great fit to the environmental stewardship theme. Ms. Wu encourages her second-graders to make text-to-text connections between Isatou's project and the "reuse" category presented in Layton's informational text, *A Planet Full of Plastic*. She also asks the second-graders to make text-to-self connections by thinking of other examples of how the actions of one person can positively affect the environment.

With younger learners, a focus on language development is key for positioning them as deep comprehenders of text. At early levels, specific constellations of unconstrained skills are difficult to differentiate. Unconstrained skills include intersections between language comprehension and other cognitive skills. Research studies (most notably a large-scale set of studies known as RfU (the Reading for Understanding project) conclude that general language abilities are difficult to distinguish, as they are interrelated with cognition, yet they are necessary to include in instruction. These intersections of unconstrained skills include background knowledge, vocabulary knowledge, word reading, inference making, and use of strategies. Later success in text comprehension includes proficiency in these areas, especially in the ability to make inferences. RfU researchers also point to expanded vocabulary, morphology, awareness of syntax, and text organization in support of teaching for deep comprehension (Cervetti et al., 2020).

Comprehension depends on background knowledge and experiences, as well as the reader's awareness of the situation in which the text is meant to be used (Cervetti et al., 2020). To successfully prepare children as deep comprehenders, it is necessary to create high-quality language experiences, These happen in environments where words and their multiple components (semantics), and complex language structures (syntax), are encountered frequently. Through such environments, children are exposed to, and encouraged to use, written and oral language often as they transact with texts (Gaméz, 2020). Teaching through a transactional view builds literacy as a set of practices where oral language is a key component.

Teachers who provide rich experiences with texts include specific instructional moves that embrace language development. This type of instruction reflects a mindset that reading is not only inclusive of but also goes beyond the marks on the page. As such, rich experiences with texts that tap students' background knowledge, engage students' motivations, expand vocabulary, introduce knowledge about how texts are constructed for different purposes, and create opportunities for students to begin to develop metacognitive awareness about their own reading practices are necessary components of early literacy instruction (Wright, 2018/2019).

Types of Dialogue: Value of
Dialogic Interactions Around Text

Classroom talk is key to fostering deep connections with meaningful texts. Teachers who support learners as deep comprehenders engage them in specific types of *extra-textual* or *analytic talk*. They create dialogue around ideas in texts with the purpose of collaboratively constructing meanings (Wright, 2018/2019). In analytic talk, language is the vehicle through which readers learn higher order thinking processes. This type of interaction around a text is more than asking students to retell a story or recall facts. Retelling is a common way to assess text comprehension, yet retelling assesses only surface-level meaning. Research on early literacy teaching indicates that much of the questioning in early childhood classrooms is limited to surface comprehension where a teacher, as expert, presents information and then asks students to follow prompts that require recall (Garcia et al., 2011). This type of teaching resembles a testing situation rather than an invitation to connect and build new ideas. Deep comprehension requires more of teachers and learners.

Analytic talk is one classroom practice that invites students to connect their own experiences to evidence in the text through open-ended discussion (where a preset response is not expected). This does not mean that teachers simply ask questions and accept any and all student comments. Instead, analytic talk requires an understanding of several factors that students need to develop to become independent, deep comprehenders. One factor that can be nurtured through talk is students' metacognition. That is, talk can help students develop awareness of their own learning. When students develop metacognition, they self-appraise and monitor their reading to make decisions about meaning. This is known as *executive control* and it is a key evidence-based finding related to effective comprehension. Such control can be gained when children are taught to articulate *what they are learning, how they are learning*, and *when and why they are learning* (Fang & Cox, 1999).

Teachers who engage with students in analytic talk can help make learning visible. For example, when Ms. Wu uses vocabulary from her environmental unit and invites students to discuss examples of how they *recycle* or *reuse* materials; she is providing metacognitive talk to support students as they explore and build cognitive understandings of new language. When she invites students to discover how they can make connections to the text, she names the strategy and points out how they can use connections to build their ideas about helping the environment.

MAKING MEANING THROUGH VOCABULARY DEVELOPMENT

Vocabulary development is crucial to deep comprehension and knowledge building, each of which is central to the fundamental purpose of all literacy activity—meaning making. Building vocabulary is essential to children's literacy development and must not be put off until children can decode proficiently. Rather, to effectively support children's literacy development, they must be engaged in robust word learning simultaneously with learning the codes of language and engaging in dialogue around concepts and ideas found in texts and in their worlds.

Learning Vocabulary: What Does It Mean to Know a Word?

Children begin learning language and rich vocabulary quite naturally from the first months of life, as they listen to and engage with family members around daily rituals and activities in the home. Most families don't consider the number of words their children learn during this time if they are functioning successfully as a member of the family unit. However, the quantity of words children know may become a measuring stick for literacy development when they begin formal schooling. This is due, in part, to an influential study published by Hart and Risley in 1995. These authors reported that families who live in lower socioeconomic communities speak less with their children, and therefore, their children's vocabulary size is smaller than that of children from more privileged families. This study has been widely cited and used to blame families, especially families of color, for low literacy development. Despite compelling critiques of a flawed research methodology, the report's influence and the belief that there is a lack of language in homes reinforces deficiency views of children and families, as well as deficiency beliefs that shape assessment and instructional practices used in schools (Dudley-Marling & Lucas, 2009; Gorski, 2012; Souto-Manning & Rabadi-Raol, 2018).

When children enter schools, their word knowledge is often measured with arbitrary lists or, in the early grades, pictures of words deemed appropriate for their grade level. Words from such lists are disconnected from meaningful contexts and thereby discount learners' family and community experiences through which they make meaning. Assessments like these may be used to label children based on the number of words they "know," or their breadth of word knowledge, with little to no consideration of the quality, or depth, of that knowledge (Hadley & Dickinson, 2020). Researchers have been critical of measuring vocabulary, an unconstrained skill, based solely on numbers of words, or *breadth* of word knowledge (Hadley et al., 2015; Wesche & Paribakht, 1996), instead, seeking to understand more about children's *depth* of word knowledge, as depth of word knowledge is more closely associated with deep comprehension (Ouellette, 2006).

Vocabulary *depth* is a learner's richness of knowledge about individual words. Perfetti and Hart (2002) refer to the complex process of developing word meaning as the *lexical quality hypothesis*. That is, *knowing* a word involves the seamless integration of the phonology (sounds in the language), orthography (the written text), and semantics (meaning) of the word. Incomplete, or missing, information in one or more of these constituents results in a low-quality lexical representation. For example, when reading about a birthday party, young children who have been engaged in learning the codes of language may be able to "sound out" and pronounce a word like *gather* but lack semantic knowledge about the word needed to understand its meaning. In this case, a reader would need a reference that in some cultures, it is common to come together (gather) with family and friends each year to celebrate the day of a birth.

Because children vary in the quality of their lexical representations, there are different levels of knowing words that make word knowledge difficult to measure with discrete assessments. Beck, McKeown, and

Kucan (2013) identified levels of knowing a word from no knowledge to a rich decontextualized knowledge of a word's meaning, including its relationship to other words and metaphorical uses. This means that children benefit from multiple encounters with a word across time and space; with each encounter deepening their knowledge of the word. Extending the previous example, a young child may "know" the word *gather* in the context of play; specifically, cleaning up after play, as in, "Let's *gather* up all the blocks and put them back on the shelf."

Children's lexical representations for words grow in quality when they are exposed to words in multiple contexts and have opportunities to use them in meaningful conversations. Let's briefly return to Ms. Wu's reading of *One Plastic Bag: Isatou Ceesay and the Recycling Women of the Gambia,* where she stops to invite her students to engage in meaningful activity to better understand some figurative language.

MS. WU'S CLASSROOM: PART THREE

Ms. Wu stops after she reads this sentence, "Rain drums on the creaky aluminum roof." She asks, "Have you heard rain when it falls on our classroom roof? Who can make that sound?" Students eagerly snap their fingers or beat their fists on the story time rug as Ms. Wu's notices how the author uses the word, *drum* to represent that sound. Ms. Wu regularly asks students to participate in connecting to description or abstract words and phrases that she knows are part of narrative texts such as this. She is intentional in stopping to explore the description of rain on the roof. She knows the importance of helping students use participation to get a sense of the setting of the story and enter the character's world.

Through exposure and participation such as the example above, children add words to their receptive and expressive vocabularies. Children's receptive vocabularies include words they can comprehend and respond to, even if they do not yet use them in their oral language. Words that children use to convey their thoughts, feelings, and ideas make up their expressive vocabularies. It is common for children's receptive vocabularies to be larger than their expressive vocabularies.

Selecting Words for Direct Instruction

Teaching vocabulary with deep comprehension and knowledge building in mind means carefully considering which words to teach and how to teach them so that children regularly add new words to their receptive and expressive vocabularies. Researchers have identified three types, or tiers, of words based on their utility in oral and written language (Beck et al., 2013). This tiered framework was designed to support educators in selecting vocabulary for direct instruction that promotes long-term academic success.

> **Tier 1** words are basic words that most children know like *happy*, *clock*, and *dog*.
> **Tier 2** words are high-frequency words for mature language users, like *bashful*, *fancy*, or *modern*, which can be found in multiple contexts.
> **Tier 3** words are words whose frequency is low because they are limited to a specific domain. For example, *biome*, *tundra*, and *biosphere* are words that relate specifically to life science, and therefore, may only be encountered by children in their elementary science class.

There is consensus in the field that effective vocabulary instruction includes an explicit focus on academic vocabulary—Tiers 2 and 3—consisting of domain-general sophisticated words and domain-specific technical words (Zucker et al., 2021). In addition to the types of words it's important to teach, Zucker, Cabell, and Pico recommend choosing words that are essential for comprehending particular texts, accessible for children's developmental levels, and valuable for long-term reading and academic success. Finally—and particularly when thinking about teaching for deep comprehension—consider selecting for direct-instruction vocabulary words that are related to a specific concept or idea. Doing so creates opportunities for dialogue during which children can use the words they are learning to build relevant knowledge.

Vocabulary Instruction

Teaching vocabulary is complex. Given what we know about lexical representations and what it means to know a word, it's important to consider the implications of this knowledge for all vocabulary instruction. Children learn words incidentally and through direct instruction. According to Ramachandra, Hewitt, and Brackenbury (2011), "Incidental word learning is a complex process that encompasses phonological processing, memory for a novel word, and making a connection between the novel word and its referent" (p. 94). Incidental word learning typically occurs when children read complex texts independently. Because most young children read easy texts in which vocabulary is controlled to support building decoding skills, it is important to build their vocabularies through direct instruction and frequent opportunities to use the words they are learning in meaningful conversation. However, findings from research on vocabulary instruction in the early grades revealed that word meanings were typically addressed during "teachable moments" in the context of other instruction, word selection was unsystematic, and minimal time was devoted to science and social studies, curriculum areas that afford abundant opportunities to introduce sophisticated vocabulary (Wright & Neuman, 2014). Further, researchers found that teachers in economically advantaged schools explained words more often and were more likely to present sophisticated words than did their counterparts in economically disadvantaged schools.

Based on an evaluation of vocabulary programs for early learners, effective vocabulary instruction includes direct vocabulary instruction, promotes incidental word learning through interactive read-alouds and independent reading, and fosters word consciousness (Zucker et al., 2021). Word consciousness means being aware of and interested in words, their meanings, and how they are used. Children who are word conscious are motivated to learn and use new words, and as such, they are more likely to develop what Hammond (2021) refers to as word wealth, which she argues is essential for equity.

Effective vocabulary instruction begins with the careful selection of words and a clear plan for introducing these words in a meaningful context. It continues with creating multiple opportunities to use them to build knowledge. For example, Ms. Wu's intentional teaching of rich vocabulary, like *biodegradable* and *microplastics*, found in quality texts includes classroom routines that value students' adoption and use of these terms. She has chosen a range of texts (known as a *text set*) to provide her students with repeated opportunities to visit and revisit key ideas about their purpose of learning about environmental stewardship. Intentional dialogue across texts deepens students' comprehension. Not only do they ask and answer questions posed by their teacher but they also connect in personal and cultural ways with the messages shared by the authors over the course of the school day, into their home experiences, and across time. Through these activities they develop their own thinking in relation to the purpose of the unit. Ms. Wu is intentional in her lessons, however she does not just read aloud to her students with the hope they will absorb information. She does not use questioning as an evaluative tool to see if students have memorized factual information. Instead, she uses the texts as tools with intentional planning. Her transactional approach to teaching aligns with current research in the field (Moje et al., 2020).

THE RELATIONSHIP BETWEEN VOCABULARY, DECODING, AND COMPREHENSION

Although vocabulary knowledge has most often been associated with the language comprehension portion of the SVR (simple view of reading) model, there is strong evidence that it also contributes directly to word recognition (Duke & Cartwright, 2021). Kearns and Al Ghanem (2019) tested third- and fourth-grade students' general semantic knowledge (vocabulary size), morphological awareness, and orthographic and phonological knowledge after reading polysyllabic words in isolation. They found that children read words better when they know their

meanings and when they understand how to use morphemes to deci-
pher word meanings. Other researchers (Kendeou et al., 2009; Mitchell
& Brady, 2013) have also found relationships between vocabulary knowledge and word recognition. This evidence suggests that quality vocabulary instruction supports learners with making links between phonology,
orthography, and word meanings, thereby facilitating the orthographic
mapping process that is essential for automatic word recognition while
simultaneously building meanings that will facilitate comprehension.
The value of robust vocabulary instruction in the early grades cannot be
overstated. As early learners engage in instruction that integrates phonology, orthography, and word meanings, they will be more likely to find
purpose and value in both learning skills and drawing on their rich cultures and backgrounds to make sense of a variety of texts.

DEEP THINKING THROUGH
INTERACTIONS WITH RICH TEXTS

Using texts to think and reason in depth depends on teaching with
materials that offer complex language and complex ideas. Regular,
supported engagement with books and other materials that stretch
learners' capacities to think and reason are important components in
intellectually rigorous literacy instruction. In the early years, interactions with these materials through read-alouds offer learners necessary
intellectual challenges that should extend to instruction throughout the
school years.

Interactive Read-Alouds

Learners develop what Zaretta Hammond calls intellectual muscles as
they participate in transactions that invite them to make meaning with
others. As adults, our role is to scaffold this process by choosing high-
quality texts and actively engaging children with the ideas brought forth
in such texts. Teachers prepare read-aloud experiences that intentionally develop deep reading. As Sandra Lennox (2013) succinctly reminds
us, "The ways books are shared may open or close learning opportuni-

ties and possibilities to use language for an increasingly wider range of purposes" (p. 381).

Ms. Wu is committed to her students' developing big ideas through literacy, and we agree that this is necessary intellectual work that is amenable to instruction. Scaffolding students' reasoning and thinking around high-quality texts is an essential component for early literacy development. Complex texts present more-stringent challenges for readers. They provide invitations to develop higher level reasoning and thinking about big ideas. One of the misconceptions present when early literacy instruction follows the learn to read and *then* read to learn model is the assumption that skill in independent decoding of words must precede access to meaningful interactions with texts. For this reason, often the bulk of early reading and writing instruction becomes oriented to decoding and encoding as we "wait" for students to be ready to understand complex texts.

Ms. Wu includes decodable texts in her instruction to introduce and practice how to unlock words. She knows that at early stages decodable texts include controlled vocabulary focused on specific phonemes and spelling patterns and simple sentence structures. She also realizes that the role of decodable texts is on decoding development. Decodable texts do not present language and content that support sophisticated reasoning processes. Therefore, Ms. Wu, and teachers like her, ensure that their literacy instruction also regularly includes the use of interactive read-alouds and text explorations that challenge learners to develop language and to engage in higher level reasoning.

The practice of interactive read-alouds is more than simply reading to children, it is reading *with* them. Regular, ongoing interactive read-alouds are opportunities for teachers to model fluent reading and higher level thinking, as they invite students' participation through analytic talk. Interactive read-alouds support students in making critical connections between their own experiences and meanings offered in a text. Interactive read-alouds are just that—interactive—all participants involved in the reading and discussing of a text are developing new ideas, even the adults. This does not mean that adults are accepting of all responses from learners without comment, but that they know learners enough to consider what they bring to a transaction and then challenge their thinking further.

WHY ARE INTERACTIVE READ-ALOUDS AN IMPORTANT PART OF LITERACY EDUCATION? Young children are capable of higher level discussion, such as that found in analytic talk, yet much of the observational research in early childhood classrooms finds that the talk centered around books, as well as the choices of books, limits learning to literal or surface-level comprehension. Leah McGee & Judith Schickedanz (2007), after visiting multiple early childhood programs across the United States, noted that most of the books found in those settings were concept books that taught basic *factual information* such as letters, numbers, or colors. Other researchers report similar findings and recommend moving talk beyond the literal.

As deep comprehension demands inferential thinking, interactive read-alouds provide opportunities for children to engage in text-based discussions where they apply ideas, compare and contrast different parts of a text or across different texts, and consider the author's purpose in writing a text and/or whether the text is effective in achieving this purpose. Important, also, is preparing readers and writers to consider multiple points of view in order to ground their opinions or make arguments (Wright, 2018/2019). Ms. Wu invests in a classroom culture where her students are comfortable with new ideas. She also values their own experiences and intentionally chooses texts that celebrate those experiences.

MS. WU'S CLASSROOM: PART FOUR

While reading *One Plastic Bag: Isatou Ceesay and the Recycling Women of the Gambia*, Ms. Wu and her students notice examples of Wolof, a language of the Gambia. Benji comments, "I am just like Isatou Ceesay. She speaks two languages and so do I." After reading, the class finds that they can learn more about Wolof through a guide to that language located at the end of the story. Ms. Wu knows that awareness about language differences is also connected to the concepts related to global perspectives. She makes a mental note to locate more books for the classroom that incorporate multiple languages.

PREVIEW, SELECT, AND USE RICH TEXTS. Big ideas are found in rich language, so the choice of texts for read-alouds is key. In keeping purpose at the forefront, the selection of texts includes a few dimensions. First, selecting texts that engage children's minds and hearts leads to motivation and interest in reading. Second, creating sets of texts around a theme, project, or unit of study challenges the intellect and presents opportunities to build word wealth. Ms. Wu intentionally chooses quality texts to interest her students in issues of environmental stewardship. She also assembles these sets of texts to include both narrative, informational, and persuasive genres all offering perspectives on the theme. Third, introducing quality texts that have potential for readers to generate big ideas, that is, to make inferences or build connections. Fourth, quality texts offer opportunities to reflect on language. These are texts that may involve multiple languages or those where the vocabulary and syntax stretch beyond learners' current lexicon. Finally, providing students opportunities for choice is key to building ownership in their learning. One activity for classrooms with regular interactive read-alouds is a "choice bin"—a box where students can place their favorite books as suggestions to be shared as group read-alouds.

TEXT TYPES AND PURPOSES. Teaching literacy as a purposeful process involves supporting learners to become active readers and writers who see themselves as text users. Experiences with a range of texts is key to understanding how texts are used for different purposes. Adults who choose multiple genres when reading aloud help learners understand how texts function to align with purposes, such as to entertain, inform, or persuade. Interactive read-alouds provide opportunities to mentor discussions about how authors achieve their purposes and build awareness important for independent use of texts across domains. Yet, these experiences are not a regular component in the early literacy curriculum. Literacy researcher Tanya Wright (2018/2019) studied 55 early education settings. She found little attention to rich narratives and no evidence of informational texts used for read-alouds. Other studies confirm that few early classrooms provide interactive experiences with informational texts. Choosing quality texts is a necessary first step in developing curriculum that cultivates deep thinking and comprehension.

In choosing texts for read-alouds there are factors to consider. For example, knowing students' interests and backgrounds is important. However, adults need to be mindful that students' identities are complex. What adults think may be a "good-fit" text for students, may not be (Osorio, 2020). As teacher educators, we spend time in our classes examining literature for the multiple ways in which young readers might connect with quality texts. For example, the picture book *A Big Mooncake for Little Star* by Grace Lin (2018) is a narrative written as a celebration of the Asian mid-autumn festival. It features a mother and her young daughter baking a mooncake for the holiday. The plot builds as the little girl cannot resist taking small bites as the mooncake cools, each bite altering the shape to resemble the phases of the moon. Many children reading these books may connect to their own cultural pride. Others may connect to a holiday celebrated with a cake that is different from their own experience. Still others might connect as they, too, have been tempted to sample bits of icing or cookies. Some might be worried about parental disapproval and then be relieved at the mother's loving response. Knowing that child readers might relate to characters or situations across different dimensions is key to book selection.

Other factors in selecting books may include themes or topics under study. For example, Ms. Wu in developing her science-themed unit on the environment selects a text-set for daily read-alouds. This set of books includes both narratives and informational texts on the topic. Providing several texts helps learners to build knowledge over time by not only answering current questions but by developing new questions. In summary, high-quality texts are "sophisticated" in that they offer a rich repertoire of vocabulary and opportunities for discussion that enhance comprehension (McGee & Schickedanz, 2007). *A Big Mooncake for Little Star* offers the latter, multiple opportunities for making inferences that range from connections between family members and feelings to building knowledge about the moon. Books such as *A Planet Full of Plastic* and *One Plastic Bag: Isatou Ceesay and the Recycling Women of the Gambia* chosen by Ms. Wu are sophisticated in that they provide disciplinary language related to the environment as well as the potential for discussion about grammar or syntax related to informational text.

An additional note concerning text types and purposes is the importance of informational texts. As we've discussed, many of the texts found in early education classrooms are fictional story narratives, thus active engagement with informational texts is a needed addition to early literacy education. Meaning making for different purposes involves multiple forms of reasoning. For example, informational texts are just that— materials through which a reader can gain information. A classroom environment that values inquiry and genuine dialogue uses texts to build new ideas. For example, while observing a first-grade read-aloud about popcorn, researchers Laura Smolkin and Carol Donovan (2003) recorded a student asking, "What is a [corn] kernel?" Rather than providing an answer, the teacher opened a discussion about finding information, "Let's read and see if this [book] answers that question?" (p. 27). Informational texts also offer grammar and overall structures specifically related to disciplines such as history or science inquiry. The research mentioned earlier on deep comprehension indicates that this knowledge of syntax and global structures support children's development of frameworks for anticipating information (Smolkin & Donovan, 2003).

A final note on selecting texts. Key to providing rich literature is awareness of our own blind spots as adult educators. At times, we share identities with our students, and at other times, we bring perspectives that differ from the experiences of the children we teach. There are many tools that adult educators can use to evaluate texts for bias. There are also critical literacy practices that are essential for developing such critical awareness in young readers. Criticality is a key dimension that informs deep comprehension and the positioning of readers as active users and analyzers of texts.

DEEP COMPREHENSION THROUGH AUTHENTIC QUESTIONING. From a transactional perspective, a rich language environment is one that scaffolds children's language a bit above their current linguistic skills (Gaméz, 2020). Interactive read-alouds provide a vehicle through which teachers use dialogue to model practices that lead to deep comprehension. Adults model by thinking aloud about content and engaging students through authentic questions. Young children do not naturally engage in analytic thinking. Supporting them as developing text analysts, therefore, begins with modeling and gradually shifts to greater student participation. The goal is for learners to develop strategies that "stick" for their own reading independence. Open-ended (how and why) questions are based on the text and/or illustrations. Learners are encouraged to elaborate on what is written in the text with their own purposes, or experiences, and to compare and contrast with other evidence across the text or between texts. Adults prepare before reading aloud, looking for opportunities to stop and to engage thinking. Rather than questions that evaluate a learner's retention of information, open-ended prompts invite discussion. An adult may help students connect by thinking aloud about the story or building on students' comments. For example, "Why do you think . . . ?" or "What must it be like . . . ?" Adult readers may ask learners to elaborate with "Say more about this . . ." or "Your response makes me think . . ." There are some teaching tools where teachers provide initial scaffolds for listening and responding to others through conversation stems. An example might be: "When you said that . . . it made me think about . . ." (MacPhee & Cox, 2019, p. 92).

When teaching story narratives, McGee and Schickedanz (2007) suggest repeating interactive read-alouds over three sessions with specific focus areas that support learner strategies for deeper comprehension. For example, younger readers are not usually sensitive to the problem posed during a narrative, so adult readers engage them in anticipating the story problem during an introductory read. This is a different technique from what our teacher education students report in their own practices. Usually, adults show the front and back cover of the book and identify book concepts such as title and author. McGee and Schickedanz recommend waiting to do this as it can distract learners from focusing on the story's meaning. During a second reading, the adult engages listeners further in analytic talk. Adult readers may think aloud with comments that explain a character's action and later ask students to explain or make inferences. Finally, a third read-aloud is recommended. At this time, learners are familiar with the story. This is a good time to examine the title and discuss details about characters' actions and/or how they relate to the goals, or problem, of the story. Inviting students to participate in reconstructing parts of the story is another recommended scaffold. A favorite activity is asking learners to "help" the adult reader by paraphrasing the dialogue. Interactive read-alouds provide a site for developing active and deep comprehension with rich texts as learners are developing decoding abilities with more-controlled texts. In sum, the goal for interactive read-alouds is activating readers' engagement and awareness of how to think and reason—the intellectual work of reading.

REASONING AND THINKING WITH TEXTS ACROSS LITERACY DEVELOPMENT

As they gain independence, learners transfer and begin to apply the reasoning and thinking modeled earlier. Efficient and effective reading is more than simply knowing the meanings of words in a text. It entails strategic processes such as *predicting based on current information, questioning and revising understanding during reading, integrating prior information, thinking aloud, using the text structure, representing ideas visually,* and *summarizing* (Duke & Pearson, 2008/2009). Recent research on teaching for deep comprehension reminds educators to be careful not to teach strategies as the "end" goal of lessons—reducing lessons to generalized strategies without seeing the point of those strategies does not orient readers toward text differences (Fang & Schleppegrell, 2010). As related to this chapter's theme, it is the purpose that guides the reading of any text and the strategies taught should always be used with purpose in mind.

Scaffolding during read-alouds nurtures emerging independence as learners engage with books on their own. The focus on reasoning and thinking with texts continues into later instruction. The practice of *close reading* is one which provides tools for students to build ideas through the use of texts. Close reading entails teaching students independent application of many of the same reasoning skills that adults have framed with read-alouds (Facing History & Ourselves, n.d.). These include determining an author's purpose, unpacking word meanings, and identifying how the text structure fulfills the purpose. It develops learners' habits of mind in bringing essential questions to their own reasons for reading. The organization *Facing History and Ourselves* describes skillful close reading as "an important foundation for helping students develop the ability [to use evidence from texts] to justify their claims in class discussions and writing assignments" (Facing History & Ourselves, n.d., para. 1). Close reading involves a protocol in which students read a text more than once, answer text-dependent questions, create visual images, share images, and then engage in discussion. Versions of this protocol can be a teaching tool enhanced by connecting prior knowledge and critical questioning to texts used in literature study, history/social studies, and science.

Another practice to assist readers' transition into deep comprehension might include book clubs or literature circles. These are literature discussions where a small group of readers engages in self-directed talk about texts, often novels. Teachers set up routines and structures for analysis and text-based discussion. Generally, book club members read sections or chapters of a novel and meet after each reading for ongoing analytic talk. Many adults who are members of book clubs realize that it is sometimes difficult to initiate and maintain focus on a text when there is so much to talk about with a group of friends. Literature circles are intended to provide elementary learners with tools for deeper focus on text while they build new ideas with others in a social context.

One helpful framework that supports developing independence in analytic talk is known as question answer relationships (QAR). QAR is a framework that can assist teachers and learners in evaluating ideas in a text through four different types of questions (Reading Rockets, n.d.).

- The first are *right-there* questions, literal questions where the answer can be found directly in the text.
- Second are *think and search* questions, where readers gather different information from the text and make inferences.
- Third are called *author and you* questions, where the reader connects evidence directly from the texts with their own experiences to answer a question.
- Fourth are *on my own* questions, which require the reader to bring their own experience or points of view to analyze messages in the text.

These are questions that tap the elements of deep comprehension. They provide teachers with a guide in which to ensure that their discussion prompts help students use evidence from the text to relate concrete ideas in service of more inferential and critical thinking.

A complementary routine that shifts independence to student readers in developing their independence in discussions is *reciprocal teaching*. Reciprocal teaching is a practice where students learn to self-direct analytic discussions. They learn four different comprehension strategies and then apply these through an assigned role in the group.

- The *questioner* is responsible for posing questions about unclear or puzzling information and noting connections to other concepts already encountered.
- The *clarifier* picks up on these questions and guides the group toward addressing them in the talk.
- The *predictor* helps the group look ahead about what will happen next based on discussion so far.
- At stopping points, the *summarizer* highlights key ideas to frame upcoming reading and future discussion.

This strategy is one of a set of what are known as instructional conversations. Recent reviews of research emphasize that teachers' implementation of these strategies is key to successful group discussions. For example, as we reminded earlier, teaching the strategies as the end goal does not lead to independent collaborative construction of coherent understandings. Dialogues are productive only when teachers scaffold by requesting students to elaborate on their ideas, redirecting meandering discussion back to the text, reworking or revoicing student contributions to connect into the discussion, and modeling strategies for students to see how they work in use (Palincsar et al., 2019).

CONCLUSION

The focus of this chapter has been on the necessity of keeping purpose at the forefront when teaching literacy. The skills of efficient reading are only productive if readers are conscious of their purposes and goals—*why* they are reading a text. Keeping purpose at the forefront disrupts the single story of learning to read *before* reading to learn. Instead, a simultaneous focus on the foundational skills for independent decoding along with intentional interactions with rich texts is the key to long-standing, effective reading for deep meaning. In this chapter, we've focused on instruction that builds vocabulary and text analysis as a process of reasoning and thinking—intellectual work. As this is a complex process, it was important to discuss how the goals of read-aloud connect across literacy development. Reading aloud is not simply a practice for early literacy education, it is useful throughout pre-K through 12 instruction. The focus on deep comprehension is also not simply a goal for reading aloud but a process—important, as readers read texts independently. As teachers and teacher educators, we need to examine our knowledge of what counts as comprehension and how we are (or are not) helping learners develop these practices.

CHAPTER 4

Building Competence and Confidence

Learners who have positive literacy identities see literacy as an active process and themselves as agents who use the language arts to achieve goals important to them and their lives. Learners with positive literacy identities also see themselves as capable. Although literacy identity is linked to success in school and in life (Afflerbach, 2022), it is something that isn't visible in the learning standards or easily assessed through standardized tests. Yet, a learner's sense of being smart is integral to how they respond to instruction as well as how, and if, they move toward

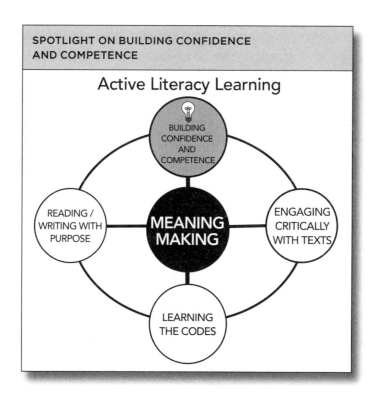

SPOTLIGHT ON BUILDING CONFIDENCE AND COMPETENCE

Active Literacy Learning

BUILDING CONFIDENCE AND COMPETENCE

READING / WRITING WITH PURPOSE

MEANING MAKING

ENGAGING CRITICALLY WITH TEXTS

LEARNING THE CODES

literacy independence. Confidence in one's ability shapes cognitive development. It is necessary that we as teachers create learning contexts that are responsive to students' assets—the resources they bring to the classroom. Valuing these resources challenges learners to stretch intellectually. Let's visit the classroom of a first-grade teacher, Ms. Crawford, who takes the time to connect with her students and their families.

MS. CRAWFORD'S FIRST-GRADE CLASSROOM

On the first day of school, Ms. Crawford chooses a special picture book, *All Are Welcome,* by Alexandra Penfold and Suzanne Kaufman, to read to her students. This award-winning book celebrates kindness, inclusivity, and diversity by following a group of children and their families as they participate in the everyday activities of school. The illustrations represent a range of dress, racial features, family members, and abilities as children work, play, and share together. The line "You have a space here" communicates safety and caring. The children eagerly point out familiar connections as they talk about illustrations in this book and other texts carefully chosen by their teacher. Ms. Crawford takes time to ask students to share and further explain their connections to the literature. Parents of Ms. Crawford's students are grateful for the ongoing contact with the teacher beyond just reports and letters home to families. Early in the school year, Ms. Crawford reaches out to each family to learn more about her students' lives outside of school. She is interested to learn that one of her students, Shara, attends church regularly followed by Sunday dinner with her grandmother. Through these reach-outs, Ms. Crawford also discovered that Shara's friend Maritza, whose parents moved from Puerto Rico, speaks Spanish at home and English in school. Upon learning that Maritza's mother takes the time to craft stories in Spanish and is teaching Maritza to read Spanish while she is learning to read English in school, Ms. Crawford invited Maritza's mother into the classroom to share the stories she and Maritza have created. Ms. Crawford regularly asks her multilingual students, who speak Spanish, Farsi, Mandarin, Vietnamese, and Black English, to add to a special wall that highlights ways with words in different languages. Ms. Crawford captures students' small successes with digital photos that are sent home when her students accomplish a new skill or take a risk and try new learning activities.

CONFIDENCE AND COMPETENCE GO HAND IN HAND

Ms. Crawford's teaching helps learners develop skills and strategies while they are also building positive identities as literate people. Her invitation to Maritza and her mother, for example, sent a message that multiple languages are valuable and valued in her classroom. By communicating regularly about her students through digital photos, and inviting family members to visit and contribute in the classroom, Ms. Crawford has created a space for learning where family members are comfortable asking questions or alerting the teacher to issues that arise outside of the classroom. Ms. Crawford also feels more comfortable communicating both successes and challenges because she has a relationship with her students' families and community. She knows that when children feel safe and seen by adults, they develop confidence to attempt new and unfamiliar academic learning tasks. In sum, she has taken the time to identify the linguistic and cultural resources of her students' families, known as "funds of knowledge" (Moll et al., 1992), and to rethink her instruction to draw on that knowledge.

However, while teachers like Ms. Crawford have worked to approach and invite these resources into the classroom, many teachers, especially those whose social, cultural, and linguistic identities differ from their students, feel they need additional support as they attempt two-way dialogues with families. An aspirational meeting is a model for educator/ family interactions based on the recognition that the life experiences of families are often the best sources of "skills and wisdom" needed to create anti-racist, anti-linguist, and anti-ableist pedagogies (Mattute-Chivarria, 2021, p. 2). This model provides prompts for gaining insights into families' hopes and dreams for their children and outlines a communication process wherein teachers actively listen while demonstrating respect, empathy, and affirmation. The process includes guiding structures for parent/teacher meetings in which the focus is on creating and recording goals as a collaborative process, drawing on the expertise of families and their knowledge of students' cultural environment and out-of-school learning. This model represents a significant shift away from traditional individualized educational planning (IEP) meetings, where the focus is on testing to uncover specific skill or behavioral deficiencies and to suggest prescriptive solutions.

Understanding and valuing different ways of knowing in relationship to the classroom curriculum is known as *asset-based* pedagogy. Instruction based on a single story sends a different message, that nondominant ways of knowing are less valuable or even invisible. Instruction based on these beliefs is known as *deficit based*. Deficit-based attitudes and practices occur when learners who don't fit dominant definitions of achievement receive interventions designed to "fix" or "cure" them. As we will see later in this chapter, such interventions, while well-intended, often have negative consequences for learners' identities and, consequently, their achievement.

[handwritten margin note: asset-based pedagogy vs Deficit-based attitudes]

THE RELATIONSHIP BETWEEN COGNITION AND EMOTION

The connection between literacy learning and identity development is becoming increasingly apparent as multiple research fields begin to exchange ideas and findings. For example, neurobiological research on literacy acquisition as an *embodied process* connects cognitive growth (which develops intellectual capacity) with social, cultural, and emotional experiences. These latter experiences are integral in determining the brain's structure. Neural networks form in relation to learning conditions. Neurobiologist Mary Helen Immordino-Yang, education leader Linda Darling-Hammond, and educational policy scholar Christine Krone (2019) explain how research on brain development equates to the complex reasoning needed for sophisticated reading comprehension. They explain that there are three major brain networks that support mental capacities: executive control, the default mode, and the salience network. Although a full accounting of all three is beyond the scope of this chapter, understanding the default mode provides one set of insights into how reading may be affected by different instructional experiences. The default mode involves internal reflective thought such as: remembering past experiences, imagining scenarios, making inferences including awareness of abstract or morally relevant information, and gaining empathy or compassion. This network is important for connecting social/emotional capacities with the cognitive.

Sophisticated reading comprehension is an outgrowth of this network that supports conceptual understanding, creativity, and nonlinear and "out of the box" thinking (Immordino-Yang et al., 2019). Because the fields of neuroscience and education use very different research methods, up to now they have rarely been used to inform each other. However, there is emerging neurobiological research that seeks to link what appear to be parallel research goals between educational/psychological research and neurobiological research. For education and psychology there are studies about "identity." For the neuroscientific fields these include questions regarding how the brain processes social stimuli. This cross-disciplinary knowledge considers how contextual (social) experiences frame cognitive development (Immordino-Yang & Gottleib, 2017).

What is currently defined in media sources as "the science of reading" is mostly based on research studies of the brain on the role of phonological processing underpinning the ability to decode words fluently—that is, the area of the brain that processes the phonology or sound systems of the language and the ability to link sounds and symbols is necessary for decoding print (see Chapter 2). This has been the basis for mandated instruction where a phonics curriculum is taught as a singular, paced set of activities isolated from meaningful experiences with texts. Ongoing research about brain development recognizes reading as a more complex activity: where processing of phonology is essential but does not operate successfully in isolation. Emerging fields in neurobiological research suggest that brain activity related to reading is a distributed set of processes along multiple dimensions.

Research on phonological processing in relation to word reading is the most well-established area of brain research related to reading. Thus, it is most prevalent in media reports on how children learn to read and how reading should be taught. However, in matters of the brain, reading is a distributed and networked process. Emerging neurobiological research indicates that reading processes are distributed across different areas of the brain and include semantic comprehension processes and embodied processes in addition to phonological processing. As these areas of the brain are activated during reading, neural networks for reading are strengthened, which increasingly contributes to reading comprehension (Compton-Lilly et al., 2020). And importantly, social and emotional experiences are central to intellectual growth. Thus, the science of reading must not limit the influence on reading instruction solely to research on phonological processing but instead must expand its reach to consider the interrelated semantic comprehension and embodied processes. Broader communication between the neurobiological and educational/psychological research fields promises fuller understandings about reading development, which in turn promises to expand our understanding of the efficacy of instructional applications.

As noted above, the context in which a person learns shapes their brain structure. Messages that students internalize about themselves as learners affect how their brains react in learning situations. Brain development is linked to feelings of well-being, safety, and connection in communities with others. There is a mind–body reaction that occurs when a person perceives that they are not considered competent within their learning environment. Such a negative message creates emotions that trigger "survival-related neural mechanisms" in the part of the brain that monitors perceived danger (Immordino-Yang & Gottleib, 2017, p. 349S). When the brain is alerted to social or physical threat, cortisol, a stress hormone, is released. This temporarily shuts down the brain's communication systems and delays higher level processing such as learning, problem-solving, and creative thinking (Hammond, 2015).

This reaction occurs when students repeatedly experience micro-aggressions such as those connected to race, ethnicity, sexual orientation, and/or socioeconomic status. It is also present when learners who are considered less capable are positioned by instruction that waters down academic expectations in light of their perceived deficiencies. Dividing students into permanent, rather than flexible, learning groups seals identities for most students. In many classrooms, students assigned to the advanced group are considered the smart students and vice versa. Students who are limited to selecting only "leveled" books are also positioned with messages about their capabilities. Another common practice—sending students with perceived deficiencies out of their classrooms for special instruction—labels those learners as "at risk" or "struggling," which in turn can elicit such a mind–body reaction. Experiencing these shutdowns over time, in school contexts where a learner is positioned as less than capable, has the destructive power to interrupt the flow of continuous learning and, consequently, the development of neuroplasticity or growth of brain matter.

Brain Development in Multilingual Learners

Another area neglected in single-story solutions to reading instruction is brain development in multilingual learners. Single-story curriculum is based on research on monolingual learners. Multilingual students develop language and literacy differently since their literacy learning and brain development involves the intersection of more than one language. Secondary language development draws on the systems already in place for learning primary language(s); therefore, learners must connect primary to additional language elements (such as vocabulary, phonological components, grammatical structures, and writing systems). Recognizing multilingual connections is essential to effectively supporting literacy development in these students. Ignoring their primary language(s) actually interferes with ongoing neurological connections important for optimizing these connections (Escamilla et al., 2022).

Thus, the contextual experiences of the learner and the biological, cultural, social, and emotional factors involved in becoming literate must be considered foundational within any instructional framework. The ALL framework supports these connections rather than any hierarchical, single-story instruction. Teachers who consider what children *are* doing and *can* do challenge deficit views of learners because they attend to cognitive development within the contexts of their students' lives, including in school. By creating positive relationships with children and families, Ms. Crawford's pedagogy supports intellectual growth as an outcome of positive literacy identities. Her understanding of the language backgrounds of her students is key to developing those positive relationships and identities.

SHIFTING TOWARD ASSET-ORIENTED PEDAGOGIES

The acts and practices of teaching espoused in a classroom or a school, and the policies related to instruction are framed through theories about how people learn. For instance, most reading curricula—including teaching guides, student texts, and assessments—are organized by grade level. Students whose progress does not meet the standardized expectations for what they are deemed to need to know at a certain age or grade stand out as in need of different and sometimes separate instruction. Interventions are delivered with the intention of shaping the individual to better resemble "typical" learners. A 2006 article in *Reading Research Quarterly* summarizes how this works in schools and identifies some of the factors that are troubling about such practices:

> Student diversity, whether socially, linguistically, or cognitively based, is primarily viewed by schools as a disability that requires segregation (e.g., placing children in settings outside of the general education classroom) and remediation. Growth in identification of individuals for special education is one consequence of this deficit perspective. Over the last decade, the number of students labeled as learning disabled has tripled, and the numbers of students designated at-risk has risen dramatically. Equally disturbing, children from culturally and linguistically diverse backgrounds

have historically been overrepresented in these special education classes and remedial programs. (Eckert et al., 2006, p. 289)

Terms such as *at risk* or the label *disorders* set up self-fulfilling expectations about learners that, once applied, are difficult to shake. When a learner becomes othered by such labels their competency is called into question. In alignment with the ALL dimension, *building competence and confidence*, the Eckert et al. quotation suggests that literacy educators must rethink the meaning of *difference* to focus on learning variability rather than individual disability. That is, instead of seeking to reshape all learners into a standard mold of ability (ableism) or cultural behaviors (racial and linguistic compliance), educational practices must recenter instruction to fit optimum ways of knowing, as Mrs. Crawford does when she invites a mother into the classroom to share stories created for her daughter at home and in her home language. Such a shift assigns competence to all students and challenges educators to better understand the practices of learners and their families. It also demands a reexamination of learning contexts in classrooms, such as grouping and leveling of students and materials. A shift toward asset-based pedagogy also implies that as educators we must first identify the practices in classrooms that continue to reinforce and repeat negative learning outcomes for many students. We must consider what recentering away from these practices means for positive literacy identity development.

Ability/DISability: Moving Away From a Medical Lens

Three student populations most excluded from mainstream education in America are consistently cited in discussions concerning the "achievement gap." These are African American students, English learners, and students identified as disabled (Annamma et al., 2018; Escamilla et al., 2022; Kohli et al., 2017). The language of a gap normalizes expectations for learning development and pathologizes the learning of those who do not appear to meet these normalized expectations. Much of the language of special education draws on the medical metaphor we described in the introduction of this book where nondominant learners are positioned as possessing an individual pathology, similar to a disease. Something inherent in the learner must be "treated." Treatments are designed to assist the learner in completing learning tasks the same way as their peers who are deemed nondisabled. Treatment goals that rely on deficit pedagogies (i.e., refitting learners into normative expectations) might include requiring all students to answer questions with standard responses, work independently to complete predetermined classroom learning tasks, develop nondisabled communication skills, match teachers' expectations for behavior, and engage in traditional discourses for making friends (Park et al., 2021). Shifting away from deficit-focused goals does not mean denying psychological or biological differences among learners but instead acknowledging the effects of cultural, political, and economic practices on learning (Waitoller & Thorius, 2016). Asset-based learning environments disrupt normative goals and instead look to create instruction that views all learners as "whole people with their own needs, desires, and purposes" (Park et al., 2021, p. 41).

Author Pat Paugh has seen examples of both asset- and deficit-focused literacy instruction in her frequent visits to elementary classrooms. Her university is located in proximity to a large, urban school district, where school funding is generally focused on success in passing high-stakes testing. Practitioners are always aware that poor test performance will lead to school takeovers by the state department of education. Thus, the mentality of "fixing" what is wrong with teachers, students, and families predominates the instructional focus in many of the schools. Interactions with exemplary elementary literacy teachers illuminate the realities and challenges of sustaining asset-based practices in school systems largely grounded in deficit-based ways of thinking and being.

In one elementary school, a first-grade teacher implemented a curriculum that included both decoding instruction as well as rich language development through interactive read-alouds. At first glance, the curriculum provided instruction that supported our framework for ALL, because it included early skills development using a systematic decoding curriculum alongside rich meaningful interactions with high-quality children's books. However, frequent standardized testing was also embedded in the school practices. When such testing revealed that students were not meeting the benchmarks for grade-level decoding, a large chunk of time was set aside to pull students from their regular classroom instruction for "intervention blocks." The amount of time necessary for these separate blocks interfered with the ability of the teacher to engage in meaningful interactions during read-alouds, leaving the teacher feeling frustrated that rich vocabulary and higher level discussions of complex texts fell by the wayside for many of her students.

This instructional intervention follows the medical model: separation of learners who don't learn at the pace of the mandated curriculum into "treatment" groups outside the classroom. Separating students in this way leads to lowered expectations for their learning and is a form of invisible *tracking*, in which students removed from the regular classroom are denied intellectual rigor. Asset-focused classrooms, instead, consider how learning variation might be addressed differently. Switching from a deficit perspective to an asset perspective may require that teachers and schools reconsider an appropriate mix of instructional practices for the particular students in their care, rather than taking oppositional stances about the one best way to teach all children, as is characteristic of reading wars arguments. For example, acknowledging the need for explicit decoding instruction for many early readers does not mean rigid immersion in a paced curriculum for all. Instead, small, flexible groups can be created to respond to frequent, teacher-focused assessment around what learners know and can do on a skills continuum. Small flexible grouping based on such "kidwatching" (Goodman, 2002) meets instructional needs and depends on teachers who understand the curriculum and their students. Reconsidering assistance in this manner might free up time for the higher level interactions with language and texts that are necessary for all learners.

Universal Design for Learning

One set of practices that is helpful in recentering asset-based instruction is universal design for learning (UDL). UDL is based on the social model of learning that insists that "any curriculum not designed with the range of student diversity in mind is in itself 'disabling'" (Waitoller & Thorius, 2016, p. 370). Designing instruction with the UDL model asks educators to consider three principles that focus on learners' outcomes rather than on how well they adapt to existing contexts (Rose & Meyer, 2002). The principles encourage instruction that provides multiple pathways to learning.

- The first, *multiple means of representation,* encourages more than one format and flexibility across formats.
- The second principle, *multiple means of action and expression,* includes planning for how learners will navigate learning activities and demonstrate what they know.
- The final principle is *multiple means of engagement,* which focuses on the learners' interests and purposes for participation in the learning—a key link to the framework for ALL, as outlined earlier in Chapter 3.

Asset-focused learning positions learners as agents. In the case of literacy, this focus includes the goal of developing a positive and purposeful literacy identity. UDL guides teachers to position all learners as *smart: experts* in what, how, and why they learn. Differences among students include learning variations related to language and culture; thus, teachers who initiate asset-based practices also include culturally sustaining pedagogies as they build instruction designed toward competence and confidence.

RETHINKING CURRENT SCHOOL PRACTICES TO AFFIRM POSITIVE LITERACY IDENTITIES

Institutional practices that lead to separation and gaps for students with disabilities, students of color, and students for whom English is not their first language are rooted in deficit beliefs around three areas. The first is *ableism*: discrimination against learners with identified or perceived disabilities. These can be physical, emotional, or learning characteristics of students that differ from what is perceived to be "normal." The second is *systemic racism*: biases that privilege white cultural norms as standard, resulting in expectations that students of color whose learning is out of sync with these norms are less capable or behaviorally disordered. The third is *linguicism*: the belief that dominant varieties of English, and related cultural ways of knowing, are superior to non-English languages and cultural practices. This deficit view extends to varieties of English such as African American or Black English. Curriculum standards, which are used to justify implementation of mandated curriculum, do not address cultural perspectives. Silence around cultural differences reinforces the continued dominance of white cultural practices as standard (Tortorelli et al., 2021). Public reforms such as the 2001 No Child Left Behind (NCLB) Act do not truly reform practice, because they preserve the status quo of inequity in educational opportunities. Anti-racist, multicultural, and culturally responsive groups in literacy education are increasingly asking for the disruption of harmful belief systems that lead to what Gloria Ladson-Billings (2013) terms *opportunity gaps*; they challenge educators to rethink deficit pedagogies and to develop relevant and responsive instruction.

Literacy instruction that honors what learners know and can do must acknowledge and leverage the linguistic and cultural assets that students bring to school. We need instructional designs based on beliefs that counter the single-story narrative and one-size solutions to reading education. The UDL principles provide one set of guidelines for educators who seek to enact asset-based instruction. There are several other helpful models based on such beliefs. One is the concept of "high-expectations" curriculum, where instruction is based on the belief that all learners are competent (Dudley-Marling & Michaels, 2012, p. 8). A high-expectations curriculum challenges learners to stretch their intellects within collaborative environments in which their expertise is included and valued. High expectations and culturally responsive instruction depends on dialogue that uncovers and builds on existing expertise.

A related concept is that of "watered-up" rather than "watered-down" curriculum (Ellis & Wortham, 1998, p. 144). Special education researchers Ellis and Wortham confront the minimized curriculum—such as the earlier example, where intervention resulted in the denial of rich read-aloud experiences. They suggest watered-up curriculum that provides:

- deeper, less superficial coverage of concepts;
- scaffolding to develop habits of mind for complex thinking; and
- interactive lessons where students are positioned to construct rather than receive and regurgitate knowledge.

Another model that links high expectations to cultural responsiveness is provided by educator Zaretta Hammond's definition of culturally responsive education. According to Hammond, culturally responsive education

- focuses on improving the learning capacity of diverse students who have been marginalized educationally,
- centers around affective and cognitive aspects of teaching and learning, and
- concerns itself with building cognitive capacity and academic mindset by pushing back on dominant narratives about people of color. (Hammond, n.d., n.p.)

Additionally, a recent review of research on literacy development for English learners/emergent bilinguals (Escamilla et al., 2022) provides findings that expand upon earlier, more narrowly focused research, such as that reviewed by the National Reading Panel (NRP). The 2000 NRP report, sponsored by the U.S. Congress, and used extensively in teacher education and assessment, ignored multilingual literacy development. The 2022 review from the National Committee for Effective Literacy (NCEL) provides a helpful set of summary findings with implications for teaching emergent bilinguals in ways that connect and develop, rather than subtract from, their existing language resources (Escamilla et al., 2022). The recommendations in the NCEL report include these statements.

1. Reaffirm the understanding that literacy embraces writing as well as reading and encompasses all five essential components of the National Reading Panel as crucial and interrelated. We build upon those findings . . . by
   a. *embracing the dual-language brain;*

    b. *scaffolding instruction for EL/EBs to bolster comprehension, participation, and language development;*

    c. *supporting oral language development as the foundation for literacy; and*

    d. *emphasizing the development of high levels of biliteracy.*

2. Insist that effective literacy instruction is understood not as a one-size-fits-all but should be specific to the needs of various groups and communities. EL/EBs require attention to their dual language brain and realities—cross language imperatives, the hopes and need for biliteracy development.

3. Call for federal and state leadership and investment in effective literacy instruction and the teachers, curriculum, and resources needed to support the instruction that EL/EBs need. (Escamilla et al., 2022, p. 14)

Enacting anti-racist, anti-ableist, and anti-linguist pedagogies requires rethinking how literacy is taught in today's classrooms. This does not mean rejection of what we know about reading development. But it does mean introducing new ways of thinking about what and how to teach. We share the particular guidelines and findings above because although they emerge from slightly different perspectives, they all hold a common message that challenges deficit-based institutional structures. This same message aligns with the guiding beliefs for our framework: that students' resources, purposes, and expertise must be integrated into challenging content. Implementing any prepackaged curriculum will never be fully effective for all learners without these considerations, and without respect for students' competence and confidence.

Designing Pedagogy That Is Culturally, Linguistically, and Socially Responsive

Educators who adopt and adapt instruction using models such as these realize that literacy identities are inherently complex. Asset-based educators do not teach to stereotypical "groups" of learners. No one identity can be considered static. Because such instruction is necessarily responsive to individual students, it is helpful to glimpse how some educators in different contexts create and adapt their teaching to engage and challenge the learners in their care. Below are two examples. The first is from a classroom research project conducted by Pat Paugh in collaboration with teacher Mary Moran; the second from the research of Dr. April Baker-Bell on linguistic justice for speakers of African American English (also known as Black English).

EXAMPLE 1: HAIR SALON WRITING. Third-grade teacher Mary Moran made sure to schedule her writing workshop (mini-lessons, independent writing, teacher/student writing conferences) to ensure that all students participated. That is, she made sure that students who were regularly pulled from the classroom for special education interventions were present. Ms. Moran shared mini-lessons using examples of procedural writing, or what students called "how-to" writing. Procedures included recipes, instructions for games, or directions for activities. During the mini-lessons, the children examined examples of recipes and instructions, and together created charts of language and text structures that fit the purpose of instructing readers on how to complete an activity. Then the class jointly constructed some how-to writing together.

For the culminating project, Ms. Moran sought to acknowledge students' interests and purposes. Students were asked to choose a topic and write a procedure independently. Nyla, a student identified as learning disabled, received most of her literacy instruction outside of class from interventionists. However, she participated fully in the writing workshop. For her written procedure, she chose to write about "washing hair." She spent a great deal of time outside of school with her African American female relatives who ran a hair salon. Familiar with the process and proud of her expertise, she constructed a procedural piece of writing that was well within the class rubric for proficient understanding of procedural language (Paugh, 2022; Paugh, 2018).

Ms. Moran's confidence that all her students could benefit from explicit teaching about language of procedure, along with Nyla's confidence in a procedure she knew well and was valued in her home community, led to competent, grade-level learning. This is one example of the benefits of access by all students to a curriculum that challenges new learning (competence) while acknowledging resources they bring from outside of school (confidence). It illuminates a student's writing development in a classroom where the teacher *watered-up* instruction.

EXAMPLE 2: DECODING INSTRUCTION WITH ATTENTION TO LANGUAGE VARIATION. Dr. April Baker-Bell's work educates the field about the rich history and complex structures of African American English/ Black English (AAE/BE), a syntactically complex language system that is frequently devalued in classrooms as a nonstandard form of English (Baker-Bell, 2020). She shares an example of a teacher who created a word wall in her classroom to include AAE/BE. The teacher translated relationships between AAE/BE and pronunciations of sound patterns encountered in students' texts. Therefore, when students are working to sound out and spell words encountered in conventional English, they can use the board to analyze cross-linguistic pronunciation of the same vocabulary. Bell states, "We're not saying that you can't teach children differences in phonology (e.g., 'dem' and 'them'), it's the way teachers are doing it" through erasing or devaluing students' language "that's troubling." (Thornton & Osborne, 2022, p. 7).

Bell makes an important distinction between what is known as "code-switching" and "register-shifting." When children are expected to switch from their primary language in ways that position dominant language as superior, their identities are threatened. On the other hand, in classrooms where students examine the use of language variations for different purposes, they are analyzing "register." All speakers and writers shift register depending on their purpose and audience. Building repertoires of language to be drawn upon depending on purpose and audience adds to linguistic power. When teachers include analysis of linguistic and text differences, they are also building cognitive power.

We chose to highlight Baker-Bell's example because AAE/BE is often ignored as an additional language. However, the NCEL review of literature on EL/EBs encourages building a "continua of biliteracy" (Hornberger, 2008) where learning contexts welcome and leverage multilingual resources across all languages with positive academic results. This teacher's word wall—a strategy that effectively embraces and leverages AAE/BE while teaching the phonological codes—is a powerful example of culturally responsive teaching that disrupts both linguicism and systemic racism.

CONCLUSION

The examples above suggest that building competence and confidence can be done in existing literacy classrooms. This requires ongoing professional learning by teachers, as well as acknowledgement of teachers' professionalism in creating high-expectations curriculum. The ALL framework emphasizes literacy instruction that builds positive literacy identities in ways that challenge learners intellectually while also engaging them in learning that is relevant and purposeful.

CHAPTER 5

Engaging Critically With Texts

Engaging critically with texts is an essential, interconnected dimension in the ALL framework. A strong literacy identity emerges when learners see literacy as something they *do*. The view taken in this book is that literacy is a verb—it is an active process where literate people engage with texts to achieve goals important in their lives. Such a stance implies that literacy is "a way of being through which to participate in the world in and outside of school" (Vasquez et al., 2019, p. 300). Critical literacy is a productive process through which people transact with texts with the

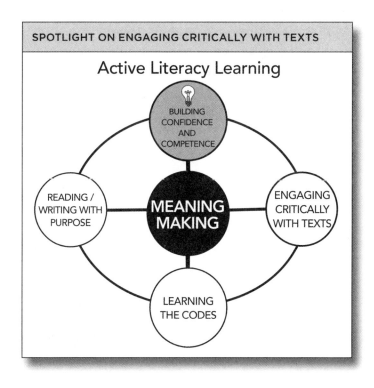

SPOTLIGHT ON ENGAGING CRITICALLY WITH TEXTS

Active Literacy Learning

BUILDING CONFIDENCE AND COMPETENCE

READING / WRITING WITH PURPOSE

MEANING MAKING

ENGAGING CRITICALLY WITH TEXTS

LEARNING THE CODES

goal of transformation. Critical literacy education values learners' experiences, languages, and cultures. This view of literacy is one in which participation is an active process of exchange rather than a passive experience where teachers deposit information into the heads of learners (Luke, 2012). As educator Gholdy Muhammad (2020) so aptly states, criticality affirms the "genius" of all learners. A critically literate person is one oriented toward a vision of justice, using texts to transform society toward social, political, and economic equity. As is evident in Ms. Guerra's classroom lesson, shared below, our youngest children are capable and engaged when they are invited to take a critical stance.

MS. GUERRA'S FIRST-GRADE CLASSROOM

Ms. Guerra takes time to consult the Common Core State Standards (CCSS) to frame her first-grade literacy lessons. To guide students' comprehension, she frequently includes a Grade 1 Reading Literature standard, "asking and answering questions about key details in a text" (National Governors' Association, 2010). For Ms. Guerra, this means more than asking students to answer assessment-type questions. She reflects on what this comprehension strategy, questioning a text, means in her classroom where literacy is conceptualized as a critical and transformative process. Ms. Guerra aims to teach students to consider not just preset messages in a text, but how messages relate to their own lives or offer perspectives that may be affirming or harmful to others in the world.

Ms. Guerra enjoys teaching with quality literature. For a genre unit focused on story narratives, she taps texts that send messages about literacy as a powerful tool for making change. These are narratives that invite children to question and consider deeper messages. One book is a fictional narrative, *Click, Clack, Moo* (Cronin & Lewin, 2000). In this humorous book, the animals in Farmer Brown's barn discover a typewriter and begin to compose notes demanding fairer treatment from the farmer. They leverage the products of their "labor" (e.g., milk and eggs) for warm blankets in the cold barn. As they examine actions of the characters (animals and the farmer), the first-graders consider themes about fairness. At the end, the animals win their demands and hand over their typewriter. Ms. Guerra wonders aloud about this action, "Was it a good decision for the animals to give up their typewriter (their literacy tool)?" Many students offer alternative suggestions, such as keeping the typewriter and sharing it with the farmer or keeping the typewriter and sharing their story with animals on other farms. Ms. Guerra then asks students to write new endings for the story with their own ideas.

The example above clarifies how a critical literacy spotlight on "asking and answering questions in a text" can be an active and transformative process. The first-graders in Ms. Guerra's class learned that critical questions can lead to new ideas. They also experienced the power of transforming an existing text after questioning whether the ending was fair to all. Critical literacy positions children early on to become active participants in the meaning-making process, rather than being passive receivers of a predetermined message contained in a text. Many educators among us consider the goal of such pedagogy necessary to preparing learners to be "literate citizens" (Comber, 2001).

WHAT COUNTS AS CRITICAL LITERACY?

The term *critical* is used differently in conversations related to literacy education. For example, *critical reading* is frequently considered to be one and the same as critical literacy. However, these perspectives that utilize the term *critical* differ in their underlying pedagogical goals. Critical reading and critical literacy can have intersecting implications when the aim is to teach students to carefully analyze texts and address messages that are relevant to living in the world today. Yet, these approaches emerge from distinct theoretical and philosophical roots, which imply very different definitions of what it means to be fully literate. To echo the introduction above, critical literacy instruction is always designed as a process of dialogue at the intersection of power, social injustice, and the transformation of society. It is a process of participation in the world through the word (Freire & Macedo, 2005). Critically literate readers and writers pose questions and problems to any text with the intention of "interrogating the status quo and challenging commonly accepted social practices" that may oppress and cause harm (Mulcahy, 2008, p. 23).

Critical literacies develop alongside the other dimensions of literacy found in the ALL framework. One reason for uncertainty about what it means to be critical stems from various perspectives about what counts as effective literacy education. From a critical literacy perspective, educators view literacy as a transactional process between text, reader/writer, and author. This infers a dialogue where meaning is made through the interactions and intention of the reader, whose focus is on meaning that impacts social good. Therefore, meaningful engagement with a text is a "process of construction not exegesis" and not "solely the product or intentions of the author" (Cervetti et al., 2001, para. 21).

Critical Reading

Critical reading places the emphasis on analytical/evaluative thinking and creative thinking/critical thinking. When engaging in critical reading, a person reflects on their own thinking in disciplined ways, they develop tools to analyze text-based ideas in a rational and clear manner (Paul & Elder, 2005). The *Massachusetts Curriculum Framework for English Language Arts and Literacy* (Pat's home state) defines "critical approaches to analysis" as two main activities for engaging with complex texts:

> **formal analysis or close reading**—examining word choice and structure of complex texts, and
> **comparative analysis**—analyzing by comparing to other texts and looking for similarities and differences between them— may include examining the historical, political, and intellec-

tual contexts of a work along with the author's biography. (Massachusetts Department of Elementary and Secondary Education, 2017)

Teaching text analysis through this approach aims to develop the intellectual muscles to read deeply. Close reading of text is one practice where readers are taught habits of mind to gather knowledge from within a text or across texts. To meaningfully comprehend a text, a close reader defines the purpose for reading and methodically examines the structure of a text, asks and answers "text-based" questions with evidence from a text. For advocates of what is known as "new criticism" theories of literary analysis, close reading is designed to gain fixed meanings that exist in the text (Hinchman & Moore, 2013). Agreement on where the meaning exists is the difference between advocates of critical reading and critical literacy.

Critical Literacy

Critical literacy embraces the intellectual work of critical reading with an important epistemological distinction. As mentioned above, critically literate readers who transact with texts construct knowledge as part of the transaction. Critical literacy is not about uncovering knowledge that exists within a text (static meanings) but engaging in a dialogue with a text or writing and rewriting a text with the idea that knowledge is a process of ongoing dialogue. Knowledge from this perspective is less about personal accumulation and more about shared understandings within and about the social context. Critical literacy is also about rethinking or revising knowledge that contributes to social good. Probably the most helpful set of understandings come from Lewison et al. (2002) who offer four ways to recognize critical literacy.

The first is that critical literacy "disrupts the commonplace" by leading to new ways of seeing the everyday world. Readers and writers use literacy to ask about the history of subjects of study or how the messages in a text position the user of that text. Critically literate people also study how language shapes beliefs and seeks ways to critique and introduce new language of possibility and hope. A very simple but powerful example can be found in how gender is represented through assigning the colors *pink* for girls and *blue* for boys. When author Pat was teaching first grade, one of her male students chose a pink marker to draw with in art class. This caused all sorts of disruption as the other little boys informed him that pink was a "girl" color, and he should not use it. Quite upset, the entire class, boys and girls, began to argue and debate this issue. The next day, many of the male teachers in the school visited the class wearing their pink shirts or ties. The adults affirmed that pink was an acceptable choice for all, much to the relief of many students in the class.

A critical literacy perspective invites questions and discussions about unexamined beliefs such as this. Behind this seemingly simple event, are questions of value. For example, "Is it considered less valuable to be a female or represent oneself as one gender?" Do certain opportunities align with such representations? In the local Target store, there is a shelf of LEGO building toys. Some of the building sets have pink blocks and packages. On closer look, these are structures with domestic themes such as a doll house. A critical literacy discussion would ask, "Is it okay for males to be interested in caring for children or decorating the kitchen?" Young children are receiving messages from the social world all the time. Critical literacy positions them to notice, question, and think differently.

The second critical literacy concept is, "interrogating multiple viewpoints," which concerns understanding across perspectives—one's own and others'. Interrogating multiple viewpoints includes noticing whose voices are valued, and whose voices are missing when reading texts. This aspect of critical literacy encourages readers to contrast competing narratives and construct "counternarratives" that challenge dominant stories and introduce new ways of seeing the world. Critical literacy classrooms value difference as a vehicle for developing greater understandings about the world. An example is a teacher we know who was concerned with hearing her fifth-grade students' disrespectful interactions with each other. Of concern to her was that this lack of respect was leading to bullying, especially in a class with students who represented different nationalities and religious beliefs. She intentionally prepared a set of lessons around the children's book *The Sandwich Swap* by Rania Al-Abdullah. The plot of the story concerns best friends whose food choices—peanut butter and hummus—reflect their family cultures. This difference in opinions about which is better leads to a fight between them. The plot concerns the characters and their classmates considering how small differences can lead to division. The book also provided the teacher an opportunity to invite students to contribute their own experiences and ideas for resolving disputes among them. In current times, when religion, race, and/or cultural differences are the substance of divisive social media, preparing young children to question and consider multiple points of view is an essential literacy skill.

Interrogating multiple viewpoints is closely connected to Lewison et al.'s third critical literacy concept, "focusing on sociopolitical issues." Critical literacy prepares students to be literate citizens who participate knowledgeably in social and political decisions—the essence of democracy. Using literacy to this end is more than accepting all points of view. Critical literacy focuses on the power relations involved in which perspectives dominate, which do not, and which remain invisible. A second-grade teacher researcher, Wendy Seger, shared an example of how she centered her writing instruction within a critical literacy framework (Gebhard et al., 2007). At the time, she was being held accountable for teaching her students (many of them new to English) to successfully perform on a high-stakes state writing test. Ms. Seger faced a dilemma—how to provide language instruction to support their reading and writing in English with responsive instruction that was more than test preparation. Taking a critical literacy stance, Ms. Seger noted a situation at her school that students felt passionately about. Afternoon recess had been canceled at the school to make time for test preparation limiting students' opportunities for free movement during the day. Ms. Seger asked the students to write about their situation. Many, including her English learners, composed statements that included both print and drawings. She noted that several students, when writing their passion, included language features such as punctuation (many exclamation points) and accurate syntax usually missing from their test-prep writing exercises.

A critical literacy practitioner, Ms. Seger saw the opportunity to center her writing instruction in an authentic context. She framed a set of lessons with their own texts as the focus. The class first considered how the writing might address their problem. They then chose an audience, revising their drafts as letters to the school's principal requesting the reinstatement of recess. Revision of the letters included focus on formal registers that would convince an administrator to consider their proposal. Upon receipt of the letters, the principal responded with direct feedback on aspects of their writing and process that were convincing to him. He also negotiated a recess time if the students agreed to an alternative time in the day to prepare for the test. Engaging in critical literacy practices, Ms. Seger created high-expectations instruction that engaged her students in using writing for transformative action—creation of a healthier school context.

Lewison et al.'s fourth critical literacy framework is "taking action and promoting social justice." This fourth element includes the concept of analyzing how language works and using it critically to "cross borders." An example of one theoretical and practical border in schools is created by beliefs about language variation. *Translanguaging* is a theory of language that multiple language types and forms, such as English and Spanish, are not learned and processed by users as separate entities. Instead, language[s] work as a dynamic process that make up a user's "repertoire" of language available for creating meaning (Garcia & Kleifgen, 2020). This includes not only what we recognize as different languages such as the above, but also modalities like signs and symbols. Examples of the latter might include recognizing or using particular symbols, pictures, photos, diagrams that can represent a message.

Translanguaging theory also encourages the interrelationship of reading and writing, dissolving another instructional "border" we see in many classrooms. Translanguaging opens transformative opportunities for rethinking classroom practices where nondominant languages remain unrecognized and undervalued. In many U.S. schools, English is the target language for learning to read and write. The focus on English, when reduced to "English only," serves to obscure and/or devalue the rich language resources brought by multilingual students. An example of promoting social and linguistic justice is introducing younger students to opportunities to interact across languages. There are quality picture books offering examples of translanguaging, and one with bilingual themes and multiple languages is *I love Saturdays y domingos* by Alma Flor Ada (1999/2002). In this book, the protagonist celebrates her two sets of grandparents—one side with Mexican heritage, speaking Spanish and the other, European American, speaking English. In the text, both languages tell the story, with the narrator inserting dialogue and vocabulary to fit her interactions with the different grandparents. A critical literacy teacher takes advantage of this bilingual text to notice and celebrate the child's easy shifting between languages as she delights in spending time with her *Grandma and Grandpa* on *Saturdays* and her *Abuelito y Abuelita* on *los domingos*. Incorporating multilingual texts into interactive read-alouds is just one of many translanguaging practices. Translanguaging pedagogy introduces texts that acknowledge bilingualism as the language of many students (Osorio, 2020). These are pedagogies that cross the borders created by "one language at a time" beliefs (Garcia & Kleifgen, 2020, p. 555) to challenge dominance and separation of language in classrooms. Translanguaging practices are critical literacy practices with opportunities to reposition multilingualism and to model the power of language to create new ways of being in the world.

MAKING SENSE OF CRITICAL READING AND CRITICAL LITERACY IN PRACTICE

The aim of the ALL framework is to provide insights along all the dimensions of knowledge vital to developing literacy instruction. In Chapter 3, we argued for instruction with rich texts that challenge readers' comprehension of complex ideas. A practice such as close reading offers a set of guidelines for teachers who seek to scaffold intellectual work necessary for deeper reading of such texts. At the same time, this practice, while aimed at developing readers' deeper understanding, is sometimes communicated as a means to find only one "truth" in the text.

This is a very different purpose than teaching readers to interact with text in order to rethink, transform, and seek justice in the social world. A teacher interested in the latter can choose close-reading tools such as the following:

- Reflective reading, and asking:

  What can you already infer about the author of this text?
  How is the text structured?
  Does this structure make it easy or difficult to make meaning?
  Does this structure tell us anything about the author's style or purpose?
- Responding to text-dependent questions that can only be answered by referring to evidence in the text.
- Creating visual images and participating in a Gallery Walk to discuss and compare images created by other readers. (Facing History & Ourselves, n.d.)

At the same time, these tools can be infused with teachers and students practicing a critical literacy stance as they engage with the text. This latter stance would *not* expect a status quo interpretation of the text, but thoughtful questioning and rethinking of the message of the text with possible reinterpretations. Questions and connections from a critical literacy stance might include:

- Who is writing this text?
- What is the author's point of view?
- Is this author reliable?
- What are they trying to say to me?
- What messages or perspectives are *not* included in this text?
- What connections do I make to my own experiences in the world or to other texts I've encountered?
- Who benefits from the messages in this text? Who might be harmed?
- Can or should this text be revised, and for what purpose?

These questions not only benefit learners. They are useful to teachers as they design literacy instruction. The questions above are helpful to educators because they prompt careful consideration of existing curriculum resources, online professional resources, and/or media messages in the interests of learners in their classrooms. The professional practices of such educators are also critical literacy practices. The professional role of educators is an active process of design rather than passive, technical, and limited to single-story implementation. Ms. Seger, highlighted earlier, is a great example of an educator who by centering her teaching within a critical literacy stance actually provided more-effective writing instruction.

MAKING SPACES FOR CRITICAL LITERACY

A critical literacy classroom is designed as a "site of belonging" (Souto-Manning et al., 2021) where learners encounter texts to affirm their own identities and perspectives, as well as challenge themselves with the introduction of other worldviews. Critical literacy also affords "spaces of possibility," where students learn to "author their identities within the context" of their classroom community (Lanza, 2020, p. 40). Critical literacy educators Barbara Comber, Annette Woods, and Helen Grant (2017) describe the classroom as a site where everyday lives take place. Another well-known critical literacy educator, Vivian Vasquez (2004) describes the critical literacy learning environment in this way:

> *A critical literacy curriculum needs to be lived. It arises from the social and political conditions that unfold in the communities in which we live. As such it cannot be traditionally taught. In other words, as teachers we need to incorporate a critical perspective into our everyday lives in order to find ways to help children understand the social and political issues around them.* (p. xiii)

Critical literacy infuses the spaces and places where everyday literacies take place. This includes classroom environments such as those fostered by Ms. Guerra and Ms. Wu; schoolrooms where teachers think their own questions aloud and invite young children to discuss dilemmas and choices. *Making text-to-self, text-to-world,* and *text-to-text connections,* students debate possible responses, and realize that there may be more than one aspect to a story. This is a process that develops complex thought. Such conversations lead to early encounters with moral reasoning and social transformation. Classrooms that encourage critical literacy over time develop learners for whom asking and answering questions becomes a habit of mind. In these classrooms, students initiate literacy practices along with their teachers.

CHOOSING TEXTS FOR PRACTICING CRITICAL LITERACY

In choosing narratives for their unit, teachers like Ms. Guerra pay attention to what students are asking about, events that may be happening locally or in the world, and/or themes that affirm or offer new perspectives on their students' life experiences. Listening carefully, teachers notice that children are constantly talking together about events in their community. These might include affirming events such as a recent World Series win by their local sports team or more unsettling news such as reports about their local neighborhood school being closed the next year. Children are also witnesses to an ever-changing larger world. Recently, families fleeing war in Afghanistan have arrived in U.S. cities and are attending U.S. schools. Students may want to learn more about these new members of their community. They may have their own family stories about moving from places outside the mainland United States. Critical literacy educators see the power of stories for making sense of the world and consistently include critical engagement with relevant stories as central to their literacy instruction.

A teacher like Ms. Guerra gathers multiple narratives with themes about using literacy to make sense of living in the world and transforming it for the better. Some of these might be the realistic nonfiction story: *Malala's Magic Pencil,* or fictional picture books such as *Island Born* (Diaz, 2018), *The Rooster Who Would Not Be Quiet* (Agra-Deedy, 2017), and *The Name Jar* (Choi, 2003). In all of these, the protagonists use their voices, through speaking, reading, and writing, to work for change. Two of these books, while written in English, also feature other languages (Spanish, Korean). In all, the goal in choosing and using these texts is to teach students how to take a critical stance in their analysis and use of texts.

Creating a critical literacy classroom involves choosing texts with attention to content as well as modality. In terms of content, representations of culture, race, family membership, gender roles, sexual orientation, religion, life circumstances, and geographical settings are just a few of the topics of importance to young learners. There is a growing awareness about how perspectives are represented in children's literature, especially from educators with expertise in critical literacy. Despite growing calls from educators for literature that highlights issues of race, gender, LGBTQ+, and ability, there is still a dearth of children's books with authentic representation of these identities in characters and authorship. Widely cited studies of this problem are conducted every few years by the Cooperative Children's Book Center (CCBC) at the University of Wisconsin (Cooperative Children's Book Center, 2022) Their findings indicate that the publishing industry has far to go (Corrie, 2018).

Summaries of the CCBC data are revealing. Between 1994 and 2017 only 13% of children's books contained multicultural content (despite the fact that 37% of the U.S. population are people of color). The good news is that more recently these numbers are rising (28% in 2016 and 31% in 2017). However, authenticity in authorship is still lagging. In 2017, Black, Latinx, and Indigenous authors combined wrote only 7% of new children's books. It is problematic that identities important to a diverse society are not represented or are misrepresented (such as a majority of white authors writing about characters of color) in the literature available to children. There is still a long way to go in terms of authentic representation from nondominant voices in the publishing industry (Corrie, 2018).

A well-cited and helpful metaphor for assessing books conducive to the practice of critical literacy is that of books as "mirrors, windows, and sliding glass doors" (Bishop, 1990). That is, children have access to books that are: *mirrors*, or books where they see their lives reflected and valued, *windows* where they have the opportunity to engage with other lives and experiences, and *sliding glass doors*, where they are invited to participate in transforming texts and the world across perspectives. For educators (and families) seeking to increase access to diversity of content in children's texts, there are inventories available to assess existing book collections.

One of many helpful (and recent) sets of guidelines for assessing book collections is an online resource, *5 Ways to Audit Your Classroom Library for Inclusion* (Nguyen, 2021). Adults and children can look for books that feature: people of color as the central character, LGBTQ and gender-expansive characters, characters from nontypical family backgrounds, as well as characters representing usually marginalized members of society (such as those incarcerated, who are treated with dignity). Guidelines also recommend looking beyond representation to uncover subtle yet harmful stereotypes, to question gender roles, or to honor language and cultural heritage.

In alignment with the focus of the ALL framework, selecting books should include sensitivity that avoids deficit framing of diversity. It is helpful to always consider who has authored a book and whether characters or situations are framed as true to life and relevant to society. There are multiple sites for locating quality multicultural and multilingual children's books. In our literacy education classes, we recommend preservice teachers explore book awards such as the Coretta Scott King Award for African American authors and illustrators, and the Pura Belpré Award for books that celebrate Latinx cultural experiences (see Table 5.1). The American Library Association (ALA) sponsors these and many other awards including the long-standing Randolph Caldecott Medal that recognizes an artist of a distinguished American picture book, and the John Newbery Medal for the most distinguished contribution to American children's literature. There are also awards from the International Board on Books for Young People (IBBY), which offers web resources for international children's books. The ALA sponsors many additional awards in categories relevant to celebrating diverse identities. In addition, there are other organizations such as We Need Diverse Books that sponsor the Walter Awards for literature that promotes "meaningful diversity" (see Table 5.2).

TABLE 5.1

SELECTED AWARDS FOR CHILDREN'S LITERATURE

Award	Description	Link
Coretta Scott King Awards	Given annually to outstanding African American authors and illustrators of books for children.	https://www.ala.org/rt/emiert/cskbookawards
Pura Belpré Award	Presented annually to a Latinx writer whose work best portrays, affirms, and celebrates the Latinx cultural experiences.	https://www.ala.org/alsc/awardsgrants/bookmedia/belpre
American Library Association/Association for Library Service to Children (ALSC)	Book and Media Awards Website	https://www.ala.org/alsc/awardsgrants/bookmedia
The Walter Awards (a.k.a. Walter Dean Myers Award)	Recognizes diverse authors whose works feature diverse main characters and address diversity in a meaningful way.	https://diversebooks.org/programs/walter-awards/
Randolph Caldecott Medal	Awarded annually by American Library Association to the artist of the most distinguished American picture book for children.	https://www.ala.org/alsc/awardsgrants/bookmedia/caldecott
John Newbery Medal	Awarded annually by American Library Association to the most distinguished contribution to American children's literature.	https://www.ala.org/alsc/awardsgrants/bookmedia/newbery

TABLE 5.2

ORGANIZATIONS OFFERING CRITICAL LITERACY RESOURCES

Organization	Description	Link
Association for Library Service to Children (ALSC)	A division of the American Library Association, it is the world's largest organization dedicated to the support and enhancement of library service to children. Offers multiple professional resources to advocate for better services and materials for all children.	https://www.ala.org/alsc/aboutalsc
Doors to the World: Tools for Teaching Global Literacy	A partnership of educators that supports teachers' use of global literature and provides critical global experiences for their students.	http://doors2world.umass.edu
International Board on Books for Young People (IBBY)	Represents an international network of people who are committed to bringing books and children together.	https://www.ibby.org/about/what-is-ibby
We Need Diverse Books	A nonprofit grassroots organization that advocates essential changes in the publishing industry to produce and promote literature that reflects and honors the lives of all young people.	https://diversebooks.org
Learning for Justice	Formerly Teaching Tolerance, it upholds the mission of the Southern Poverty Law Center. Offers free educational resources to help foster shared learning and reflection.	https://www.learningforjustice.org/about
Colorín Colorado	A bilingual site for educators and families of English language learners providing free research-based information, activities, and advice.	https://www.colorincolorado.org/about

Locating quality literature at these sites can guide teachers to authors who offer outreach helpful to teaching with their books. For example, authors Jacqueline Woodson, Grace Lin, and Jason Reynolds are authors of color whose books have all received the John Newbery Award from the National Library Association (among many other awards). Woodson and Reynolds also have served as National Ambassadors for Young People's Literature engaging in outreach virtually and in person to young readers. All three offer multiple resources through their professional websites that can be accessed by teachers and students (see Table 5.3). Learning the stories of these and other authors offer mirrors, windows, and sliding glass doors for the preservice teachers in our classes who see the power of books for creating a powerful literacy curriculum.

As this volume supports an expanded view of literacy for the 21st century, it is necessary to consider multimodal texts as part of critical literacy instruction. This range of texts might include digital sites where authors choose and assemble messages using multiple modalities such as a web cartoon with sound; a video or a game; interactions involving

TABLE 5.3

SELECTED AUTHORS, AWARDS, AND WEBSITES

Author	Awards	Author website
Jacqueline Woodson	Newbery Medal, Lambda Award for Lesbian Fiction, Children's Literature Legacy Award, National Book Award, Coretta Scott King Award, National Ambassador for Young People's Literature 2018	https://jacquelinewoodson.com
Jason Reynolds	Newbery Medal, NAACP Image Award, Carnegie Medal, Audie Award for Middle Grade Title, Edgar Award for Best Adult Fiction, National Ambassador for Young People's Literature 2020	https://www.jasonwritesbooks.com
Grace Lin	Newbery Medal, Caldecott Medal, Children's Literature Legacy Award	https://gracelin.com

spoken and signed language; news video; and of course books, magazines, and advertising that involve printed words and images. As mentioned earlier, with the example of pink and blue branding of the LEGO building sets, advertisements on toy boxes can be a source of critical literacy conversations. Preparing young learners to interrogate how texts are constructed to persuade, positions them to be critical and informed adults as they engage with multiple text forms that increasingly surround us in today's world.

CRITICALLY READING AND WRITING TEXTS AS A HUMAN RIGHT AND A COMPLEX CHALLENGE

Young children are capable of developing powers of reasoning and empathy, yet attention to critical dimensions of literacy is not always visible in early age classrooms (Comber, 2001). Some reasons for this are underlying beliefs in young children's "innocence" and the need to be protected. Yet, as indicated by young children's noticings and questions such as those in Ms. Guerra's class, they are more than aware of power relations in their everyday lives (Comber, 2001; Lewison et al., 2015). Many children personally experience unfairness and inequity from young ages. Educator Shamaine Bazemore-Bertrand (2020) writes of her dilemma when one of her fourth-grade students shared concern about news that the U.S. government was building a border wall to deter immigrants. With no prompting from the teacher, one day her student announced this news and shared her fear that family members might be deported. Bazemore-Bertrand did not address this situation at the time as she worried about engaging in political discussions with her young students, yet in retrospect she realized that this student and others are paying attention to the news and have concerns about how events might affect them.

As we write this book, there are growing calls for censorship of topics and literature across our nation's schools. This is an issue of civil rights, the rights of students to read and write texts that affect them, their families, and their lives. The National Council of Teachers of English (NCTE) offers insights through an open letter to all in the United States concerned with the content of texts in schools. In the letter the organization relates the rights to literacy content as integral to what the United States honors as our democratic ideals:

> *The right to read, like all rights guaranteed or implied within our constitutional tradition, can be used wisely or foolishly. In many ways, education is an effort to improve the quality of choices open to all students. But to deny the freedom of choice in fear that it may be unwisely used is to destroy the freedom itself. For this reason, we respect the right of individuals to be selective in their own reading. But for the same reason, we oppose efforts of individuals or groups to limit the freedom of choice of others or to impose their own standards or tastes upon the community at large.*
>
> *One of the foundations of a democratic society is the individual's right to read, and also the individual's right to freely choose what they would like to read. This right is based on an assumption that the educated possess judgment and understanding and can be trusted with the determination of their own actions. In effect, the reader is freed from the bonds of chance. The reader is not limited by birth, geographic location, or time, since reading allows meeting people, debating philosophies, and experiencing events far beyond the narrow confines of an individual's own existence.* (NCTE, 2018, The Right to Read)

This quote from the *NCTE Position Statement on Students' Right to Read* is a companion piece to their statement on *Students' Rights to Write* (NCTE, 2014). Both of these express concern over movements to limit students' access to texts based on the religious, political, and social beliefs of others. Critical literacy education positions learners to address all texts and use intellectual and moral tools to interrogate them. Both NCTE statements elaborate the nuances for selecting, using, and creating texts based on the context of instruction. In conjunction with these statements, educators can seek support in enacting a critical literacy classroom through many educational resources.

In light of censorship, teachers face difficult decisions when enacting critical literacy instruction. There are multiple political and contextual decisions to be made as educators seek to create literacy education that is responsive and equitable. There is definitely not a single solution to what these decisions entail. However, in these times, teachers who work as collectives focused on their own classrooms as well as on the political contexts of their schools, communities, and states provide each other with support and power. An example of collective professional development can be found in the inquiry work of an educational collective in New York City shared in a volume edited by early childhood educator Marianna Souto-Manning. This group, aligned with the NCTE statements above, worked to investigate critical literacy theory and enact projects based on a cycle of critical inquiry (Souto-Manning, 2020). The group of classroom teachers, facilitated by Souto-Manning, interrogated problems in their literacy instructional practice. Their reflexive process of inquiry design is shared in that volume (see Souto-Manning, 2020, p. 109). Briefly, the group:

- individually enacted inquiry-driven *thematic investigations*, identifying issues of oppression in their classrooms;
- collectively *identified generative themes* across their practices;
- *coded* these themes;
- dialogically chose themes to *pose as problems* for collective inquiry and investigate history and roots of the problems at hand;
- dialogically *considered multiple voices and perspectives* to understand the complexity of the problems posed;
- devised informed *plans of action* for addressing these problems; and
- engaged and reported *actions* taken.

As just noted, enacting critical literacy practices is dependent on multiple factors and can never be conducted through a scripted curriculum. However, there are numerous examples available for educators to witness how tools of critical literacy and inquiry-based teaching practices have been put into action. For example, the edited volume cited above includes exemplar chapters written by teachers who participated in this New York City project.

Another example of reflective practice leading to action evolved when Shamaine Bazemore-Bertrand, the former fourth-grade teacher, mentioned earlier, moved from classroom teacher to teacher educator. She continued to be troubled by her inaction regarding the student who worried about deportation. She realized that students' literacy practices are necessary to helping them live in the world. Along with her preservice teaching candidates, Bazemore-Bertrand problematized and then investigated how children's books can be central to empower new teachers and their students to engage in important dialogue using texts on social issues. She writes of developing a safe and welcoming classroom culture early in the year using the picture book *All are Welcome,* by Alexandra Penfold (see Chapter 4 vignette featuring Ms. Crawford for additional examples using this text). This book became a starting point for inviting close relationships with students and families to identify issues that might pose difficult but necessary themes for literature discussion. For example, in addressing student concerns about immigration and deportation, the picture book *Dreamers* by Yuyi Morales shares the story of an immigrant woman and her son in America. The themes in the book celebrate hopes for a new life in a new country. The book opens doors for students to share their own family experiences and/or learn about experiences different from their own. Bazemore-Bertrand shares some prompting questions that are helpful for inviting what can often be difficult conversations. When reading *Dreamers* some prompts might be

- In the story, the woman says that she and her baby made it to the "other side." What do you think is the other side?
- Why do you think people choose to come to the United States?
- In the story, the woman shares how there are so many things they did not know. She goes to a library where she finds out new things. Where could she go in your community to find out new things? (Bazemore-Bertrand, 2020, p. 24)

Relationships with students and families serve as guides to critical literacy instruction, especially for teachers whose backgrounds and experiences differ from the children and families they teach. At other times, teachers who share nondominant backgrounds can also offer safe spaces for families to reflect on their own experiences and aspirations for their children. Relationships are powerful sources to inform classroom teachers about perspectives and are essential aspects of a critical literacy curriculum. As an example, Eliza Braden, Valente' Gibson, and RoKami Taylor-Gillette (2020) share the mutual benefits afforded when Gibson, a Black male teacher, and Braden, a Black female literacy researcher and school partner, engaged with families in discussions about literature related to Black culture and experiences, literature that Mr. Gibson was simultaneously teaching children in his literacy class. Discussions around one of these books, *Grandpa, Is Everything Black Bad?* By Sandy Lynn Holman (1998) opened doors for talk about race that they had little opportunity to share elsewhere. Conversations based on discussions of books used in the classroom allowed parents space to share their own issues as parents recognizing Black beauty and pride, along with challenges in preparing their children to navigate a racist world. The importance of a teacher of color as supportive of their own roles as parents was highlighted in the exchange.

Dialogue with families and invitations to share inside and outside the classroom can also prevent teachers of all backgrounds from making assumptions that extend stereotypes, while also informing teachers of the questions being asked and in need of answers by all their students. Trying to fit book titles to instruction without insider knowledge of students' actual experiences can cause more harm than good and is antithetical to critical literacy practices.

CONCLUSION

For us, authoring this chapter on critical literacy illuminated the interrelationships between the four dimensions in the ALL framework. Classrooms that promote critical literacy value literacy as an active, dialogic, and transformative process where students are trusted as competent knowers. Knowers are considered as agents who understand how languages work in order to decode print, and who determine purposes for what they read and write. By this time, we hope you have also noticed these connections across the four ALL dimensions. Critical literacy is the key to connecting the intellectual work of investigating meaning when reading texts, as well as writing for purposes that lead to generating knowledge that then leads to social good. In this chapter, we emphasized that critical literacy requires intellectual work and moral reasoning leading to social transformation. Critical literacy is the dimension where the early emphasis on texts with rich language and ideas includes idea generation on themes important to students' lives and world experiences. We urge educators who value this dimension to be critical literacy practitioners who ask and answer questions about social transformation as they adopt or create curriculum for teaching young learners.

CHAPTER 6

Teaching Reading Is a Political Act

In this final chapter, we recognize teaching, particularly the teaching of reading, as a political act. In doing so, we aspire to the position that teachers are professionals who must be persistent in accessing a wide range of knowledge to inform effective literacy instruction that is responsive to the many stories of their students. In addition, the role of a teacher involves negotiating the politics surrounding teaching children to read and write. To be clear, we recognize that teachers are knowledge generators and advocates for their students. This is not currently the dominant way teachers are viewed in the United States. We speculate that this might be a contributing factor in the current teacher shortage. Teachers' expertise has been bypassed in reform efforts that position them as technicians who should implement programs with fidelity, rather than as professionals who study their craft and teach responsively to the diverse needs of their students.

Our primary intention for writing this book is to move beyond single-story conceptualizations of what it means to teach young children to read and write. Often driven by the media, such conceptualizations have fueled the reading wars for decades, promoting conflict and hindering conversation that can serve to advance effective teaching and learning by connecting basic research findings and contextualized classroom practices (MacPhee et al., 2021). We intentionally avoid controversial terms such as *whole language*, *balanced literacy*, and *structured literacy* that seem to trigger conflict. Rather, throughout the book, we encourage readers to consider a broad knowledge base that is important for educators teaching children who are learning to be literate. Our ALL framework highlights four interrelated dimensions of knowledge that encompass cognitive skills and strategies, as well as affective, sociocultural, and critical domains necessary for providing all children a comprehensive early literacy education.

We hope that we have demonstrated the importance of looking within and across these domains of knowledge when considering how best to instruct and support early literacy learners. We conclude this chapter and the book by strongly advocating for teachers as professionals and agents of change, because we know that despite instructional practices or programs, it is highly educated and caring teachers that make the critical difference in education (Duke et al., 2016).

THE POLITICS OF TEACHING READING

When we refer to the teaching of reading as a political act, we mean that, historically, literacy teachers have never had full control over what, or how, they teach children to read and write. Instead, reading curriculum and instruction have been shaped by political forces, often with ambitions toward privileging methods, or even programs, of instruction that promote a single story. Teachers, then, are compelled to work under mandates and accountability measures that limit their instruction, interfere with their ability to directly respond to their own students, and spark fear about what may happen if accountability criteria aren't met.

An explicit national example of this is the No Child Left Behind (NCLB) Act of 2001. The federal policy, which placed strict mandates on what and how reading could be taught, was based on the National Reading Panel (NRP) report (2000), a review of research authorized by congressional mandate. Although we agree that classroom instruction should be guided by research, as demonstrated in our framework for ALL, we argue that a *broad range* of research is necessary to inform instruction that is effective for all students. This was not the case with the NRP report. Rather, the NRP reviewed research only on "topics for which there existed a sufficiently large pool of 'potentially viable' experimental studies" (Pearson, 2004, p. 228). These topics included phonemic awareness, phonics, fluency, vocabulary, and comprehension. This limitation on research topics and methods focused exclusively on cognitive aspects of reading—excluding, or erasing, relevant topics within affective, sociocultural, and critical domains that we know affect literacy learning. Further, it has been argued that much reading research has "idealized the U.S. student as English dominant, middle to upper class, with above normal abilities, and White" often discarding studies that "included students who were: Black and lived in urban areas, Spanish dominant learning to read in English, and low income" (Willis, 2019, p. 399).

In this case, narrowing the research that was acceptable for review by the National Reading Panel to only experimental studies was a political act that shaped through NCLB what counted as reading (phonemic awareness, phonics, fluency, vocabulary, and comprehension). There are benefits to knowledge found in this report, yet requirements to directly link it to federal funding of specific curriculum and instruction for all learners through the Reading First Act, resulted in no measurable improvement on students' reading comprehension (Gamse et al., 2008; Manzo, 2008). Reform efforts such as NCLB continue to be linked to funding for limited commercial programs and result in schools and teachers becoming dependent on preset curricula. Specific approaches to curriculum continue to be associated with the reform through media reports, advocacy group support, or in some cases, actually written into law. For example, a recent *New York Times* article (Goldstein, 2022) about the effects of the pandemic on reading achievement cites one foundational reading program complete with a link to the program's website as something states can spend federal stimulus money on. Curriculum programs that receive this kind of attention are adopted and used widely even though we know that "different kinds of reading difficulties require different approaches to instruction. One program or approach will not meet the needs of all students" (International Dyslexia Association, 2018, p. 7). The consequences of political actions like these can linger for decades, even, as was the case with reading after NCLB, when they have little effect on student learning as defined by standard measures (Dee & Jacob, 2011). Dee and Jacob, who examined the National Assessment of Educational Progress (NAEP) scores of fourth- and eighth-grade math and fourth-grade reading prior to and during NCLB, found that although "NCLB generated large and broad gains in the math achievement of fourth-graders and, to a somewhat lesser extent, eighth-graders," they found "no consistent evidence that NCLB influenced the reading achievement of fourth-graders" (p. 442).

Teaching reading isn't just political at the national level. Politics surrounding how reading should be taught can be found at the state, district, and school levels as well. For example, under pressure from organizations like the International Dyslexia Association (IDA) and National Council on Teacher Quality (NCTQ), many states have introduced legislation that aims to impose sweeping mandates on how schools assess young children to identify those perceived to be at risk of experiencing difficulty in reading, as well as on how universities educate future teachers of reading. When written into law, such policies often limit, or mandate, assessments and programs that can be used to teach literacy. Districts and/or schools then have processes for adopting curricula and expectations for implementing it, both of which have instructional implications for teachers (Valencia et al., 2006). Once programs are adopted, it is common for professional development to prioritize curriculum implementation over continued teacher education.

Reform efforts in reading education often privilege curriculum mandates and punitive accountability measures over more comprehensive improvement plans that take contextual factors into consideration. Woulfin and Gabriel (2020) critique reform efforts that promote "a microlevel, individualistic approach focused solely on teachers and their knowledge" (p. S110). They advocate for interconnected, contextualized infrastructure for improving reading instruction that is concentrated on three pillars: curriculum, professional development, and leadership. They are clear that when thinking about improvement in this way, "reform efforts will look different in different contexts and that no single approach . . . is likely to lead to instructional improvements across contexts" (p. S114).

Because the politics surrounding literacy education are complex and impact the day-to-day work of teachers and children, it is important for educators at all levels to be aware of what is happening politically within their immediate contexts, as well as more broadly. In this way, we can become agents in shaping literacy learning and teaching, and be advocates for the students we teach. And in doing so, we must always remember that it's not the instructional methods, or programs, that make the biggest difference in children's learning. Rather, it's a knowledgeable and caring teacher who has professional autonomy to design curriculum to meet the needs of the students in their classroom and in the context of their school.

TEACHERS MAKE THE DIFFERENCE

In 1985, the National Council of Teachers of English's (NCTE) Commission on Reading produced a report titled *Becoming a Nation of Readers*. The purpose was to provide a thorough synthesis of current knowledge on reading and the state of the art and practice of teaching reading. The authors of the report made two claims:

1. The knowledge is now available to make worthwhile improvements in reading throughout the United States.
2. If the practices seen in the classrooms of the best teachers in the best schools could be introduced everywhere, improvement in reading would be dramatic. (p. 3)

More specifically, the commission recognized that, according to research, "about 15 percent of the variation among children in reading achievement at the end of the school year is attributable to factors that relate to the skill and effectiveness of the teacher," while only about 3% was "attributable to the overall approach of the program" (p. 85).

In the late 1990s, the U.S. Department of Education and the U.S. Department of Health and Human Services invited the National Academy of Sciences to establish a committee to examine the prevention of reading difficulties. Contributors to the report, *Preventing Reading Difficulties in Young Children* (Snow et al., 1998) also asserted that quality instruction is the "single best weapon against reading failure" (p. 343). Although we take issue with the war metaphor (we don't think teachers should be characterized as weapons), we do value the finding and its contribution to the weight of the evidence on this matter.

Despite strong evidence that the method, practice, or program for teaching children to read is less important than the knowledge and skill of the teacher, education policy still favors what Duffy and Hoffman (1999) called the "perfect method" myth. Citing research across four decades, they argue that "it has been repeatedly established that the best instruction results when combinations of methods are orchestrated by a teacher who decides what to do in light of children's needs" (p. 11). Unfortunately, policies focus on mandating programs and materials (and sometimes training in those programs), rather than creating investment in teacher-generated knowledge about the diverse range of practices used by effective classroom teachers. These policies send the message to teachers that they cannot be trusted to make instructional decisions for their students. Such policies undermine the profession in their efforts to control teachers by positioning them as technicians. They also place the blame on teachers when one-size curriculum mandates continue to fail.

Effective Practices in Literacy Education

Duke, Cervetti, and Wise (2016) examined literature on literacy teacher quality. Specifically, they reviewed case studies of high-quality literacy teachers and established a list of more than 20 practices used by "teachers who have demonstrated unusually positive impacts on students' literacy learning, in comparison to their peers . . ." (p. 36). We first want to acknowledge their findings that effective teachers *are responsive* (p. 41) and *connect with students' homes* (p. 42) because these findings support a central argument of this book: That to effectively support the literacy development of young children, teachers must access and welcome students' funds of knowledge into classrooms and plan and implement instruction that is responsive to them.

We review below some of these practices that align with the dimensions in the ALL framework. A complete list of effective practices identified by Duke et al. can be accessed in their article in the *Journal of Education*. We hope you notice, as we did, that although we matched effective practices with particular dimensions, the practices also cross dimensions, demonstrating the interrelatedness of dimensions in the framework.

LEARNING THE CODES. In their review of what effective teachers do, Duke et al. (2016) concluded that *effective teachers teach explicitly* (p. 42) and *use assessment and observation to inform their instruction* (p. 41). In Chapter 2 you met Mr. Hall, a first-grade teacher, who, through careful observation, noticed that his students possessed a range of knowledge in phonological awareness and phonics and concluded that he was likely not meeting all students' needs through his whole-class instruction. He had recently engaged in professional development in phonological awareness and phonics and was using his new knowledge to interpret formal and informal assessment data to form small groups of students for explicit phonics instruction. Mr. Hall grew in his effectiveness as a reading teacher by engaging in professional learning and incorporating new knowledge into his instructional practice. He involved students in metalinguistic awareness by talking about how these codes worked in the text the children were decoding, and he left space to talk about the sound systems in other languages. When children are *learning the codes*, teachers *formatively* assess what they know and can do for the purpose of planning focused and explicit instruction to broaden and deepen their knowledge. This is especially important and should be done with word-level, sentence-level, and text/discourse–level codes.

READING AND WRITING WITH PURPOSE. Particularly relevant to *reading and writing with purpose*, Duke et al. (2016) found that *effective teachers are purposeful* (p. 41), as Ms. Wu is in her selection of texts for an environmental unit planned to build students' content knowledge and motivate them to become environmentally responsible citizens (see Chapter 3). Additionally, Ms. Wu selects related vocabulary to explicitly teach throughout the unit, providing many opportunities for students to incorporate new words through discussions during interactive read-alouds. We would add that along with being purposeful in instructional decision-making, effective teachers also demonstrate to their students that reading and writing are purposeful practices and not universal skills that can be applied in the same way to any text.

As well as being purposeful, *effective teachers teach for depth* (Duke et al., 2016, p. 41). Teaching for depth means engaging students intellectually through analytical talk that leads to deep comprehension. Importantly, this must happen as children learn the codes of written language. Waiting for children to master the codes before expecting them to think deeply disrupts their literacy development and can undermine the confidence they need to become competent readers and writers.

BUILDING CONFIDENCE AND COMPETENCE. According to Duke et al. (2016), effective teachers *emphasize effort* and *promote self-regulation* (p. 42). For this ALL dimension, emphasizing effort is linked to careful scaffolding of intellectual work that challenges students' thinking. Through these high expectations, effective teachers "convey a sense that all students are capable as learners when effort is put forth, and they attribute students' success to their effort as well as their ability" (p. 42). When teachers expect students to be capable learners, students begin to see themselves that way. Supporting students in developing positive literacy identities is key to their becoming agents in their own learning— choosing and using literacy to achieve goals that are important to them. In Chapter 4, we introduced neurobiological research that emphasizes the relationship between cognition and emotion. This research is bringing to light how confidence shapes cognitive development and in turn, builds competence. As children gain confidence, they feel safe to stretch themselves cognitively, becoming more and more independent and self-regulated. Ms. Crawford, who you met in Chapter 4, supported Shara in this way by valuing her linguistic and cultural resources and including them in the day-to-day activities in the classroom.

ENGAGING CRITICALLY WITH TEXTS. In Chapter 5, you met Ms. Guerra, a teacher who designs instruction that supports students' critical literacy. Critical literacy is teaching reading and thinking with a stance toward social justice. Duke et al. (2016) found that effective teachers *focus on higher order thinking skills* and *teach for equity* (p. 41). Ms. Guerra believes that teachers must be active designers of curriculum. Rather than moving passively to the next lesson in the published curriculum, it is her responsibility to reflect on her students' existing knowledge in relation to the content being taught. She takes time to review curriculum to select (and adjust) materials and activities in ways that will engage learners and position them as agents who question, rewrite, and transform texts in the interest of social good. As a critical literacy practitioner, Ms. Guerra is always mindful of her own values and biases as she engages in this work. She carefully selects read-aloud texts and tries to be open to students' questions and responses during literature conversations, as opposed to expecting fixed responses based on her own perspectives. She seeks to develop relationships that invite students and families to be part of shaping the curriculum content to keep learning connected to their interests and lives.

THE TEACHING PROFESSION

It is our sincere hope that our framework for ALL and the information contained in this book expand the personal practices of educators who choose to engage with it. In addition, when we acknowledge that teaching reading is a political act, we must also consider our roles outside classrooms. As increasingly more laws are passed that aim to control what teachers can do in their classrooms, teaching professionalism is increasingly endangered. This is reflected in the current national teacher shortage. Although reasons for the teacher shortage are varied and complex, the Learning Policy Institute recently reported that due to widespread devaluing of the profession, prospective and practicing teachers are choosing different careers (Kini, 2022). The report cited federal data on teacher attrition, which showed that "test-based accountability was the single largest reason given for leaving the profession" (para. 3), leaving no doubt that policy is taking a toll on our profession.

The impact reading policy has had and continues to have on teaching, including how policy positions teachers and how they respond to such positioning is troubling. To improve teaching and learning, teachers must be repositioned as experts who seek out and use knowledge to engage their students intellectually and emotionally by making curriculum relevant to their lives. Although we don't claim to have a simple solution to the teacher shortage, we know it's important to join together to explore solutions and become active in reclaiming the teaching profession. We aim to start a conversation here by highlighting three stances teachers can take in an effort to improve teaching and learning and to begin the process of repositioning educators as professionals. If you find value in these ideas, then we encourage you to gather with colleagues in your schools and districts to continue the discussion and move toward responsible action.

Teachers as Knowledgeable Decision-Makers (Not Technicians)

Educational policies tend to position teachers as technicians whose role is to implement, with fidelity, programs that have been identified and selected through a political process that may—or may not—be in the best interest of all students. For example, a recent study in which researchers used a critical discourse and anti-racist teaching framework to examine student and teacher materials from a scripted K–8 language arts curriculum found that "whiteness is centered at every level of the curriculum in text selection and thematic grouping of texts, as well as through discursive moves in teacher-facing materials" (Rigell et al., 2022, p. 1). This particular curriculum has recently received attention in the media and is being considered for adoption across the United States. Given that our nation is as diverse as it's ever been and becoming more diverse all the time, we question the appropriateness of adopting such a curriculum without major revisions. Yet, it's happening, and teachers are expected to implement the curriculum despite any apprehension they may have based on the content and how students may, or may not, relate to it.

In some ways, educators have accepted this positioning, possibly out of utter exhaustion as the mandates that dictate the "what and how" of our work continue to pile up. It seems that with each new mandate, we lose some professional autonomy, and we resign to jumping through the accountability hoops that leave little time for developing our craft through knowledge generation and reflection on practice. It is in these times when it is most important to remember that effective teachers make the biggest difference for children, and that teachers have been educated to make instructional decisions based on the best available knowledge for the contexts where we teach. This means that there is not a universal knowledge about what works best for children in all contexts. Instead of passively waiting for the perfect method or program that will never come, educators must be active in seeking out knowledge that is relevant to the students, families, and communities where they teach. In doing so, it is essential to consider knowledge across the interrelated dimensions of the ALL framework.

Teachers as Investigators of Systemic Inequities and Personal Bias in Schooling Practices

A widely accepted goal of education is to close the perceived achievement gap between groups of students. This gap has also been called an opportunity gap because it refers to differences in achievement on standardized tests between white students in well-resourced schools and students of different races and socioeconomic statuses. The latter often do not have access to the same opportunities as their white counterparts. Apropos of NCLB, in addition to finding no consistent evidence that the reform had positive effects on fourth-grade reading achievement, critics have also acknowledged its "limited contributions to reducing the achievement gap" (Dee & Jacob, 2011, p. 442). This critique suggests that it was grounded in "a flawed, implicit assumption that schools alone can overcome the achievement consequences of dramatic socioeconomic disparities" (p. 443). Historically, school reform efforts (including NCLB), that are grounded in single-story narratives, or the "perfect method" myth (Duffy & Hoffman, 1999) produce evidence suggesting that one-size does not fit all. Thus, one area that needs further unpacking is the push for "standardized" instruction. In fact, one-size-fits-all reforms continue to create what Gloria Ladsen-Billings names as "generic ideas about pedagogy" where a "generic kid" represents a norm (Waitoller & Thorius, 2016, p. 5). Such beliefs perpetuate systemic inequities that privilege those who fit that norm and marginalizes nondominant groups of learners who do not.

Disrupting a system that is not serving all students well, requires teachers to become investigators of systemic inequities and unconscious bias in schooling and teaching practices. The power to change a system starts with developing awareness of the often invisible structures that support it, and then taking action to disrupt these structures. One such structure in education is that of viewing children through a deficit lens based on a medical model of education. It is so common that it's often accepted without question.

TEACHER INQUIRY AS PROFESSIONAL DEVELOPMENT

Teachers who investigate practice through a process of inquiry are generators, rather than receivers, of knowledge. They position themselves and their work with students, families, school, and community by taking up an *inquiry stance* (Cochran-Smith & Lytle, 2009). Such teachers create relationships between theory and practice where they are the central generators of knowledge in their work. Cochran-Smith & Lytle explain that this is not simply knowledge that comes from experience (*knowledge in practice*), nor is it the application of curriculum knowledge received from outside sources (*knowledge for practice*) that is so common in current professional development. Instead, teachers involve themselves in cycles of practitioner inquiry as integral to their teaching. Such cycles, both individual and collective, produce knowledge as an ongoing process of learning how to teach and continually improve upon teaching—always in relation to the context of instruction. Cochran-Smith & Lytle term this type of theoretical generation as *knowledge of practice*. Two recent examples of collectively generated teaching knowledge in literacy include the New York City research collective highlighted in Chapter 5 (Souto-Manning, 2020) and a larger scale collective inquiry for curriculum planning offered in Queensland, Australia, and Ontario, Canada (Luke, 2018).

In the New York City project, elementary teachers gathered with a shared goal of transforming their classrooms to "sites of belonging," where students exercised their rights to engage in reading and writing for social justice (Souto-Manning, 2020). These teachers, all from different elementary schools in the city, engaged in critical cycles (described in more depth in Chapter 5) of thematic investigation of the problems they faced in achieving their goals, identification of generative themes, codification of a theme for inquiry, problem-posing, problem-solving, planning, and taking action. Through their participation in these cycles of inquiry, classroom teachers developed literacy curriculum and assessed students' learning. Literacy curriculum projects that evolved from this work included:

- an early childhood classroom where teachers expanded access to children's literature beyond Eurocentric themes and provided opportunities for children to author counternarratives to traditional stories;
- infusing the writing curriculum with hip-hop genres to engage literacy participation by second- and fourth-graders;
- introducing multimodal literacies with visual autobiographies, rethinking language hierarchies through a second-grade unit on immigration; and
- investigating students' rights to trauma-informed curriculum and facilitated discussions on students pushing back on hate crimes through critical literacy.

The second example is a model for curriculum planning by teachers across the school curriculum, using Luke and Freebody's four resources model for critical literacy instruction. One of the creators of the model, Allan Luke, explains the thinking behind the model and offers a reminder that a model is not a curriculum but a way of organizing literacy learning through a critical literacy belief system. The inquiry process in this example begins by asking individual teachers to check their classroom curriculum (work programs) to see if there is evidence of teaching of the four resources model for literacy learning: coding, semantic/meaning making, pragmatics, and critical practices. Teachers consider whether and how each area is addressed, what is missing, and how lessons are taught. After this process, grade-level teams are asked to compare findings from each classroom to check for consistency and/or discuss rationales for differences in units of study or lesson plans, creating a whiteboard chart. An example might be, "here is what I do with coding." Finally, charts are shared across the grade levels to invite discussion, decisions, and ongoing use of evidence to examine how literacy practices are taught throughout the school. This inquiry process, more structured and connected to a theoretical model, enables teachers to systematically study their schools' teaching and learning and evaluate how it best fits the mission, values, and effectiveness of students' literacy development (see Luke, 2018). This is a much different stance from professional development that "trains" teachers to enact sequenced and paced curriculum with a single trajectory for all students to follow.

SUGGESTIONS AND QUESTIONS FOR ACTION-ORIENTED INQUIRY

We invite readers to begin your own inquiries with colleagues. You can critically examine the programs and practices within your school or connect with colleagues who share similar questions about literacy learning across sites. The information shared through the ALL framework is intended, not as a curriculum to be applied, but as a source of information to consider as you plan and implement instruction that is responsive to students. You will not find a simple solution to literacy learning or teaching in the pages of this book. That is because there is no single curriculum or story to serve as a blueprint for teaching all children to read and write. What you will find is a wealth of knowledge, generated through systematic research across paradigms, that you can consult as you investigate problems that present themselves in your teaching practice, theorize solutions, and develop instruction that engages students and through which they grow as literacy learners.

We end this chapter (and our book) with two sets of prompts that may be helpful for guiding professional learning through collaborative inquiry and for encouraging and supporting families and community members to engage in conversations about literacy learning in class-rooms. The latter set was developed because we have heard from many families that, when they speak with teachers, are often at a loss about what questions to ask and what they need to know about their child's school experience. Finally, there is a lot to learn about engagement and transfer of learning from the learners themselves. In other words, is any-one asking the kids? Although we do not have formal prompts for this purpose, we highly recommend engaging learners in ongoing dialogue about what works for them, what they are learning, and what sugges-tions they have for ongoing design of instruction that meets their needs.

Reflective Prompts for Educators

This set of reflective prompts is intended for educators (teachers, princi-pals, teacher educators) who wish to design or revise literacy instruction in a classroom, school, or district, or to work with others such as commu-nity members or policy makers to communicate about quality literacy instruction.

REFLECTION ON LEARNERS. The central issue for teaching literacy is planning and implementing instruction that is responsive to learners. This can be done most effectively by knowing and valuing their home and community knowledge as assets to learning.

- How do we learn about the students in our classrooms? What do we know about them socially, culturally, emotionally, racially, physically, linguistically, intellectually?
- How do we get to know about learners' interests and life experi-ences? How do we use this knowledge to teach them?
- Do we talk about students in the same ways we would talk about our own children and family members?
- How could we improve our knowledge of learners?

REFLECTION ON ASSET PEDAGOGIES. One theme threaded through this book is the need for a shift from a medical model of education to a social model in which addressing students' learning based on what they know and can do is privileged.

- Are the programs and practices in our schools grounded in asset perspectives or deficit views of children? Is the first question leading to gathering evidence about learners "What *can* they do?"
- What types of evidence support students as capable learners?
- How do we design instruction to build on learners' capabilities?
- Does our instructional language reflect asset or deficit perspectives? What small changes can we make to disrupt deficit beliefs and language?

Note: Pay particular attention to deficit language that adults (and children) use to describe learners—some problematic terms to listen for in the school talk are learner designations such as *levels* or *sped students* or *behavior kids*.

REFLECTION ON CURRICULUM. When a paced, sequenced, and leveled curriculum defines what counts as success, there will always be learners who don't fit the norm. Many of these learners are assigned identities as deficient. There is a need to rethink curriculum design so that learners' assets can be privileged when implementing curriculum.

- What are our goals for effective literacy learning in school?
- What do we want to know more about in order to adapt existing curriculum or create new curriculum to stretch our readers and writers to their next steps as learners?
- Are the literacy programs in our school meeting the needs of all the students in achieving these goals?
- What aspects of, and for whom, does the literacy curriculum work? What evidence do we have for the effectiveness of the curriculum? For which students is it not working? What knowledge do we need to improve instruction for those students in ways that build their skill development, keep them challenged intellectually, and foster positive literacy identities?

- How are we adapting sequenced and paced programs to be culturally, linguistically, and intellectually responsive to different types of learners?

REFLECTION ON ADVOCACY. Classroom curriculum and instruction are frequently determined based on decisions made by policy makers who are not always experienced or fully informed about literacy learning. It is incumbent on practitioners to be prepared to educate, communicate, and advocate for those they teach.

- What do we know about the funding for literacy education in our district and school? Is it equitably funded in order to provide the resources that our students need to be successful?
- Where can we learn about literacy policy initiatives at national, state, and local levels?
- How can we effectively communicate our knowledge about literacy learning and teaching to educational leaders and lawmakers?
- Are there professional organizations and/or advocacy groups that we can join or form to grow and share our knowledge?
- How can we get family and community members to join us in our advocacy work?

Reflective Prompts to Share With Families and Community Members

This related set of prompts is for educators to share with family or community members who wish to talk with their teachers and principal and to better understand home/school connections to literacy instruction in their children's classrooms.

- Is my child excited about learning to read and write?
- What makes them interested in reading and writing?
- Have I taken time to notice what my child is doing when they are reading a book?

- Make a list of reading or writing that we do at home. Share this with your child and child's teacher.
- What are some ways that we use reading and writing (including everyday life and media) in our family? How might these support my child's understanding about learning to read and write?
- What languages do we use at home for speaking, reading, and writing?
- Please describe the ways reading and writing is taught in the classroom. What questions do I have about this?

CONCLUSION

As our book title suggests, learning to be literate is more than a single story. We crafted the title as a response to media stories that claim there's a simple solution for teaching all children to read and to blame educators for not knowing, or willfully ignoring it. It is not our intent to be argumentative. In fact, we assert that there is no solution to be found in the continued pursuit of "reading wars." We introduce the ALL framework that recognizes four interrelated dimensions of knowledge that influence literacy learning. We make a case that the single-story narrative is detrimental because its narrow focus privileges some as it harms others, perpetuating systemic inequities.

We argue that reading and writing are not universal skills that can be applied equally to all texts, but rather, they are practices that must be learned and used to achieve goals that are important to learners' lives and the world. From this perspective, it is essential that children are positioned as agents in the learning process, encouraged to engage intellectually as they learn language codes, and valued as capable learners with vast funds of knowledge. We suggest that this broader view of literacy includes attention to diversity and race, culture, and language varieties, along with multiple modes of texts.

Finally, we recognize that the teaching of reading is a political act. It is imperative for educators to be active in the political process as advocates for the children, families, and communities they serve. Advocacy is most effectively accomplished from a position of knowledge; therefore, educators have a responsibility to gain as broad a knowledge as possible of the interrelated domains that influence literacy development and to share their knowledge with families, colleagues, educational leaders, and lawmakers.

References

Adams, M. J. (1990). *Beginning to read: Thinking and learning about print.* MIT Press.

Afflerbach, P. (2022). *Teaching readers [not reading]: Moving beyond skills and strategies to reader focused instruction.* Guilford.

Aleo, T. (2020). Reading the world: A case for multimodal literacy. National Council of Teachers of English. https://ncte.org/blog/2020/01/reading-world-case-multimodal-literacy/

Allen, L., & MacNamara, D. (2020). Defining deep reading comprehension for diverse readers. In E. B. Moje, P. P. Afflerbach, P. Enciso, and N. K. Lesaux (Eds.), *Handbook of Reading Research* (Vol. 5, pp. 261–276). Routledge.

Annamma, S. A., Ferri, B. A., & Conner, D. J. (2018). Disability critical race theory: Exploring the intersectional lineage, emergence, and potential futures of DisCrit in education. *Review of Research in Education, 42*(1), 46–71. https://doi.org/10.3102/0091732X18759041

Baker-Bell, A. (2020). *Linguistic justice: Black language, literacy, identity, and pedagogy.* NCTE Routledge.

Bazemore-Bertrand, S. (2020). Classroom voices: Using children's literature to discuss social issues in the classroom. *Talking Points, 31*(2), 21–25.

Beck, I. L., McKeown, M. G., & Kucan, L. (2013). *Bringing words to life: Robust vocabulary instruction*. Guilford Press.

Bishop, R. S. (1990). Mirrors, windows, and sliding glass doors. *Perspectives, 6*(3), ix–xi.

Braden, E. G., Gibson, V., & Taylor-Gillette, R. (2020). Everything Black is NOT bad! Families and teachers engaging in critical discussions around race. *Talking Points, 31*(2), 2–12.

Bransford, J. (2007). Preparing people for rapidly changing environments. *Journal of Engineering Education, 96*(1), 1–3. https://doi.org/10.1002/j.2168-9830.2007.tb00910.x

Brisk, M. E. (2014). *Engaging students in academic literacies: Genre-based pedagogy for K–5 classrooms*. Routledge.

Brisk, M. E., & Zisselsberger, M. (2010). We've let them in on the secret: Using SFL theory to improve the teaching of writing to bilingual learners. In T. Lucas (Ed.), *Teacher preparation for linguistically diverse classrooms: A resource for teacher educators* (pp. 111–127). Routledge.

Brown, P. C., Roediger, H. L., & McDaniel, M. A. (2014). *Make it stick: The science of successful learning*. Belknap Press.

Cartwright, K. B., & Duke, N. K. (2019). The DRIVE model of reading: Making the complexity of reading accessible. *The Reading Teacher, 73*(1), 7–15. https://doi.org/10.1002/trtr.1818

Cervetti, G., Pardales, M. J., & Damico, J. S. (2001). A tale of differences: Comparing the traditions, perspectives, and educational goals of critical reading and critical literacy. *Reading Online, 4*(9). https://www.researchgate.net/profile/Gina-Cervetti/publication/334372467_A_Tale_of_Differences_Comparing_the_Traditions_Perspectives_and_

Educational_Goals_of_Critical_Reading_and_Critical_Literacy/ links/5d25e94e92851cf4407535a3/A-Tale-of-Differences-Comparing-the -Traditions-Perspectives-and-Educational-Goals-of-Critical-Reading-and -Critical-Literacy.pdf

Cervetti, G. N., Pearson, P. D., Palincsar, A. S., Afflerbach, P., Kendeou, P., Biancarosa, G., Higgs, J., Fitzgerald, M. S., & Berman, A. I. (2020). How the Reading for Understanding initiative's research complicates the simple view of reading invoked in the science of reading. *Reading Research Quarterly, 55*(S1), S161–S172. https://doi.org/10.1002/rrq.343

Chall, J. S. (1967). *Learning to read: The great debate.* McGraw-Hill.

Chall, J. S., Jacobs, V. A., & Baldwin, L. E. (1990). *The reading crisis: Why poor children fall behind.* Harvard University Press.

Cochran-Smith, M., & Lytle, S. (2009). *Inquiry as stance: Practitioner research for the next generation.* Teachers College Press.

Coles, G. S. (2000). Literacy education, democratic discourse, and psychologists. *Peace and Conflict: Journal of Peace Psychology, 6*(4), 333–338. https://doi.org/10.1207/S15327949PAC0604_04

Comber, B. (2001). Critical literacy: Power and pleasure with language in the early years. *The Australian Journal of Language and Literacy, 24*(3), 168–181.

Comber, B., Woods, A., & Grant, H. (2017). Literacy and imagination: Finding space in a crowded curriculum. *The Reading Teacher, 71*(1), 115–120.

Compton-Lilly, C. F., Mitra, A., Guay, M., & Spence, L. K. (2020). A confluence of complexity: Intersections among reading theory, neuroscience, and observations of young readers. *Reading Research Quarterly,* 55(S1), S185–S195. https://doi.org/10.1002/rrq.348

Cooperative Children's Book Center. (2022). *Books by and/or about Black, Indigenous and People of Color (All years)*. https://ccbc .education.wisc.edu/literature-resources/ccbc-diversity-statistics/ books-by-about-poc-fnn/

Corrie, J. (2018, May 10). The diversity gap in children's book publishing, 2018. *Lee & Low Books*. https://blog.leeandlow.com/2018/05/10/ the-diversity-gap-in-childrens-book-publishing-2018/

Deacon, S. H., & Kieffer, M. (2018). Understanding how syntactic awareness contributes to reading comprehension: Evidence from mediation and longitudinal models. *Journal of Educational Psychology, 110*(1), 72– 86. https://doi.org/10.1037/edu0000198

Dee, T. S., & Jacob, B. (2011). The Impact of No Child Left Behind on student achievement. *Journal of Policy Analysis and Management, 30*(3), 418–446. https://doi.org/10.1002/pam.20586

Dehaene, S. (2009). *Reading in the brain: The new science of how we read*. Penguin Books.

Dickinson, D. K., Golinkoff, R. M., & Hirsh-Pasek, K. (2010). Speaking out for language: Why language is central to reading development. *Educational Researcher, 39*(4), 305–310. https://doi.org/10.3102/0013189X10370204

Dudley-Marling, C., & Lucas, K. (2009). Pathologizing the language and culture of poor children. *Language Arts (86)*5, 362–370.

Dudley-Marling, C., & Michaels, S. (Eds.). (2012). *High expectation curricula: Helping all students succeed with powerful learning*. Teachers College Press.

Duffy, G., & Hoffman, J. (1999). In pursuit of an illusion: The flawed search for a perfect method. *The Reading Teacher, 53*(1), 10–16.

Duke, N. K., & Cartwright, K. B. (2021). The science of reading progresses: Communicating advances beyond the simple view of reading. *Reading Research Quarterly, 56*(S1), S25–S44. https://doi.org/10.1002/rrq.411

Duke, N. K., Cervetti, G. N., & Wise, C. N. (2016). The teacher and the classroom. *Journal of Education, 196*(3), 35–43. https://doi.org/10.1177/002205741619600306

Duke, N. K., & Pearson, P. D. (2009). Effective practices for developing reading comprehension. *Journal of Education, 189*(1–2), 107–122.

Dyson, H., Best, W., Solity, J., & Hulme, C. (2017). Training mispronunciation correction and word meanings improves children's ability to learn to read words. *Scientific Studies of Reading, 21*(5), 392–407. https://doi.org/10.1080/10888438.2017.1315424

Eckert, L. S., Turner, J. D., Alsup, J., & Knoeller, C. (2006). Rethinking the meaning of difference: Contemporary challenges for researchers and practitioners in literacy and language education. *Reading Research Quarterly, 41*(2), 274–291. https://doi.org/10.1598/RRQ.41.2.7

Global Education Monitoring Team. (2014). *Education for All Global Monitoring Report: Teaching and learning for all.* UNESCO Publishing. Retrieved at: https://en.unesco.org/gem-report/report/2014/teaching-and-learning-achieving-quality-all

Ehri, L. C. (2014). Orthographic mapping in the acquisition of sight word reading, spelling memory, and vocabulary learning. *Scientific Studies of Reading, 18*(1), 5–21. https://doi.org/10.1080/10888438.2013.819356

Ellis, E. S., & Wortham, J. F. (1998). "Watering up" content instruction. In W. N. Bender (Ed.), *Professional issues in learning disabilities: Practical strategies and relevant research findings* (pp. 141–186). Pro-Ed.

Escamilla, K., Olsen, L., & Slavick, J. (2022). Toward comprehensive effective literacy policy and instruction for English learners/emergent bilingual students [Report]. The National Committee for Effective Literacy. https://www.footsteps2brilliance.com/wp-content/uploads/2022/03/NCEL-Effective-Literacy-White-Paper-FINAL.pdf

Facing History and Ourselves. (n.d.). *Close Reading Protocol.* https://www.facinghistory.org/resource-library/teaching-strategies/close-reading-protocol

Fang, Z. (2012). Language correlates of disciplinary literacy. *Topics in Language Disorders, 32*(1), 19–34. https://doi.org/10.1097/TLD.0b013e31824501de

Fang, Z., & Cox, B. E. (1999). Emergent metacognition: A study of preschoolers' literate behavior. *Journal of Research in Childhood Education, 13*(2), 175–187. https://doi.org/10.1080/02568549909594738

Fang, Z., & Schleppegrell, M. J. (2010). Disciplinary literacies across content areas: Supporting secondary reading through functional language analysis. *Journal of Adolescent & Adult Literacy, 53*(7), 587–597. https://doi.org/10.1598/JAAL.53.7.6

Fisher, D., Frey, N., & Lapp, D. (2008). Shared reading: Modeling comprehension, vocabulary, text structures, and text features for older readers. *The Reading Teacher, 61*(7), 548–556. https://doi.org/10.1598/RT.61.7.4

Francis, D. J., Kulesz, P. A., & Benoit, J. S. (2018). Extending the simple view of reading to account for variation within readers and across texts: The complete view of reading (CVRi). *Remedial and Special Education, 39*(5), 274–288. https://doi.org/10.1177/0741932518772904

Freebody, P., & Luke, A. (1990). Literacies programs: Debates and demands in cultural context. *Prospect: an Australian journal of TESOL, 5*(3), 7–16.

Freire, P., & Macedo, D. (2005). *Literacy: Reading the word and the world.* Routledge.

Gabriel, R. (2021). The sciences of reading instruction. *Educational Leadership, 78*(8), 58–64.

Gámez, P. B. (2020). High quality language environments promote reading development in young children and older learners. In E. B. Moje, P. P. Afflerbach, P. Enciso, N. K. Lesaux (Eds.), *Handbook of reading research* (Vol. 5, pp. 365–383). Routledge.

García, O., & Kleifgen, J. A. (2020). Translanguaging and literacies. *Reading Research Quarterly, 55*(4), 553–571. https://doi.org/10.1002/rrq.286

Garcia, E., Pearson, D., Taylor, B., Bauer, E., & Stahl, K. (2011). Socio-constructivist and political views on teachers' implementation of two types of reading comprehension approaches in low-income schools. *Theory into Practice, 50*(2), 149–156. https://doi.org/10.1080/00405841.2011.558444

Gebhard, M., Harman R., and Seger, W. (2007). Reclaiming recess: Learning the language of persuasion. *Language Arts, 84*(5), 419.

Gee, J. P. (1992). *The social mind: Language, ideology, and social practice.* Greenwood.

Gewertz, C. (2020, February 20). States to schools: Teach reading the right way. *Education Week.* https://www.edweek.org/teaching-learning/states-to-schools-teach-reading-the-right-way/2020/02

Gibbons, P. (2015). *Scaffolding language, scaffolding learning* (2nd ed.). Heinemann.

Goldstein, G. (2022, March 8). It's 'alarming': Children are severely behind in reading. *The New York Times.* www.nytimes.com/2022/03/08/us/pandemic-schools-reading-crisis.html

Goodman, K. (1967). Reading: A psycholinguistic guessing game. *Journal of the Reading Specialist, 6*(4), 126–135. https://doi.org/10.1080/193880 76709556976

Goodman, Y. (2002). Kidwatching: Documenting children's literacy development. Heinemann.

Goodwin, A. P., Huggins, A. C., Carlo, M. S., August, D., & Calderon, M. (2013). Minding morphology: How morphological awareness relates to reading for English language learners. *Reading and Writing, 26*(9), 1387–1415. https://doi.org/10.1007/s11145-012-9412-5

Gorski, P. C. (2012). Perceiving the problem of poverty and schooling: Deconstructing the class stereotypes that mis-shape education practice and policy. *Equity and Excellence in Education, 45*(2), 302–319. https://doi .org/10.1080/10665684.2012.666934

Gough, P. B., & Tunmer, W. E. (1986). Decoding, reading, and reading disability. *Remedial and Special Education, 7*(1), 6–10. https://doi.org/10 .1177/074193258600700104

Greene, P. (2021). College and career readiness is a snare and a delusion: A look at K–12 policies and practices from a classroom perspective. *Forbes.* https://www.forbes.com/sites/petergreene/2021/02/18/college-and -career-readiness-is-a-snare-and-a-delusion/?fbclid=IwAR15VESDXimYL 2VnDfm9FICkWKBHET64bsK6dy6Njrl1jES5SoRmyGYcu5M&sh=4bd053c 51b59

Grysko, R. A., & Zygouris-Coe, V. V. I. (2020). Supporting disciplinary literacy and science learning in grades 3–5. *The Reading Teacher, 73*(4), 485–499. https://doi.org/10.1002/trtr.1860

Hadley, E. B., & Dickinson, D. K. (2020). Measuring young children's word knowledge: A conceptual review. *Journal of Early Childhood Literacy, 20*(2), 223–251. https://doi.org/10.1177/1468798417753713

Hadley, E. B., Dickinson, D. K., Hirch-Pasek, K., Golinkoff, R. M., & Nesbitt, K. T. (2015). Examining the acquisition of vocabulary knowledge depth among preschool students. *Reading Research Quarterly, 51*(2), 181–198. https://doi.org/10.1002/rrq.130

Halliday, M. A. K. (1975). *Learning how to mean: Explorations in the development of language.* (Explorations in Language Study Series, edited by Peter Doughty and Geoffrey Thornton). Edward Arnold.

Hammond, Z. (n.d.). A conversation about instructional equity with Zaretta Hammond. *Collaborative Classroom.* https://www.collaborativeclassroom.org/blog/instructional-equity-with-zaretta-hammond/

Hammond, Z. (2015). *Culturally responsive teaching and the brain: Promoting authentic engagement and rigor among culturally and linguistically diverse students.* Corwin.

Hammond, Z. (2020). Looking at SoLD through an equity lens: Will the science of learning and development be used to advance critical pedagogy or will it be used to maintain inequity by design? *Applied Developmental Science, 24*(2), 151–158. https://doi.org/10.1080/10888691.2019.1609733

Hammond, Z. (2021). *Integrating the science of learning and culturally responsive practice.* American Federation of Teachers. https://www.aft.org/ae/summer2021/hammond

Hanford, E. (2017, September 11). Hard to read: How American schools fail kids with dyslexia. *APM Reports.* Retrieved from https://www.apmreports.org/episode/2017/09/11/hard-to-read

Hart, B., & Risley, T. R. (1995). *Meaningful differences in the everyday experience of young American children.* Brookes.

Hickey, P. J., & Lewis, T. (2013). The Common Core, English learners, and morphology 101: Unpacking LS. 4 for ELLs. *Language and Literacy Spectrum, 23,* 69–84.

Hinchman, K. A., & Moore, D. W. (2013). Close reading: A cautionary interpretation. *Journal of Adolescent & Adult Literacy, 56*(6), 441–450. https://doi.org/10.1002/JAAL.163

Holman, S. (1998). *Grandpa, is everything Black bad?* Culture C.O.-O.P..

Hornberger, N. H. (2008). Continua of biliteracy. In N. H. Hornberger (Ed.) *Encyclopedia of Language and Education.* Springer.

Hruby, G. G. (2020). Language's vanishing act in early literacy education. *Phi Delta Kappan, 101*(5), 19–24. https://doi.org/10.1177/0031721720903823

Immordino-Yang, M. H., Darling-Hammond, L., & Krone, C. R. (2019). Nurturing nature: How brain development is inherently social and emotional, and what this means for education. *Educational Psychologist, 54*(3), 185–204.

Immordino-Yang, M. H, & Gotlieb, R. (2017). Embodied brains, social minds, cultural meaning: Integrating neuroscientific and educational research on social-affective development. *American Education Research Journal, 54*(1S), 344S–367S. https://doi.org/10.3102/0002831216669780

International Dyslexia Association. (2018). *Knowledge and practice standards for teachers of reading.* (Rev. ed.). Author.

Jewitt, C., & Kress, G. (2010). Multimodality, literacy and school English. In W. Dominic & J. Hoffman (Eds.), *The Routledge international handbook of English, language and literacy teaching* (pp. 366–377). Routledge.

Kearns, D. M., & Al Ghanem, R. (2019). The role of semantic information in children's word reading: Does meaning affect readers' ability to say polysyllabic words aloud? *Journal of Educational Psychology, 111*(6), 933–956. https://doi.org/10.1037/edu0000316

Kendeou, P., Savage, R., & van den Broek, P. (2009). Revisiting the simple view of reading. *The British Journal of Educational Psychology, 79*(Pt 2), 353–370. https://doi.org/10.1348/978185408X369020

Kieffer, M. J., & Lesaux, N. K. (2012). Knowledge of words, knowledge about words: Dimensions of vocabulary in first and second language learners in sixth grade. *Reading and Writing, 25*(2), 347–373. https://doi.org/10.1007/s11145-010-9272-9

Kim, J. S. (2008). Research and the reading wars. In F. M. Hess (Ed.), *When research matters: How scholarship influences educational policy* (pp. 89–112). Harvard University Press.

Kini, T. (2022, January 11). Tackling teacher shortages: What can states and districts do? *Learning Policy Institute.* https://learningpolicyinstitute.org/blog/teacher-shortage-what-can-states-and-districts-do

Kintsch, W. (2018). Revisiting the construction-integration model of Text Comprehension and its implications for instruction. In D. E. Alvermann, N. J. Unrau, M. Sailors, & R. B. Ruddell (Eds.), *Theoretical models and processes of literacy* (7th ed., pp. 178–203). Routledge.

Kohli, R., Pizarro, M., & Nevárez, A. (2017). The "new racism" of K–12 schools: Centering critical research on racism. *Review of Research in Education, 41*(1), 182–202. https://doi.org/10.3102/0091732X16686949

Ladson-Billings, G. (2006). From the achievement gap to the education debt: Understanding achievement in U.S. schools. *Educational Researcher, 35*(7), 3–12. https://doi.org/10.3102/0013189X035007003

Ladson-Billings, G. (2013). Lack of achievement or loss of opportunity.

In P. L. Carter & K. G. Welner (Eds.), *Closing the opportunity gap: What America must do to give every child an even chance* (pp. 11–22). Oxford.

Lanza, A. (2020). Students' right to author their identities. In M. Souto-Manning (Ed.), *In the pursuit of justice: Students' rights to read and write in elementary school.* (pp. 39–48). National Council of Teachers of English.

Lee, O., Quinn, H., & Valdés, G. (2013). Science and language for English language learners in relation to Next Generation Science Standards and with implications for Common Core State Standards for English language arts and mathematics. *Educational Researcher, 42*(4), 223–233. https://doi.org/10.3102/0013189X13480524

Lennox, S. (2013). Interactive read-alouds—an avenue for enhancing children's language for thinking and understanding: A review of recent research. *Early Childhood Education, 41*(5), 381–389. https://doi.org/10.1007/s10643-013-0578-5

Lewison, M., Flint, A. S., & Van Sluys, K. (2002). Taking on critical literacy: The journey of newcomers and novices. *Language Arts, 79*(5), 382–392.

Lewison, M., Leland, C., & Harste, J. (2015). *Creating critical classrooms: Reading and writing with an edge* (2nd ed.). Routledge.

Luke, A. (2012). Critical literacy: Foundational notes. *Theory into Practice, 51*(1), 4–11.

Luke, A. (2018). Critical literacy, school improvement, and the four resources model. In P. Albers (Ed.), *Global conversations in literacy research: Digital and critical literacies.* (pp. 1–13). Routledge.

MacPhee, D., & Cox, R. (2019). Interactive read alouds. In D. Stephens, J.A. Clyde, & J.C. Harste (Eds.), *Reading instruction: What, how, and why.* New York, NY: Scholastic.

MacPhee, D., Handsfield, L., & Paugh, P. (2021). Conflict or conversation? Media portrayals of the science of reading. *Reading Research Quarterly. 56p*(1), S145–S155. https://doi.org/10.1002/rrq.384

Manzo, K. K. (2008). Reading first doesn't help pupils "get it." *Education Week, 27*(36), 1–14.

Massachusetts Department of Elementary and Secondary Education (2017). Massachusetts Curriculum for English Language Arts and Literacy. https://www.doe.mass.edu/frameworks/ela/2017-06.pdf

Matute-Chavarria, M. (2021). Giving voice to aspirations: Engaging African American parents with children with disabilities. *Intervention in School and Clinic, 57*(4), 211–218. https://doi.org/10.1177/10534512211024933

McGee, L. M., & Schickedanz, J. A. (2007). Repeated interactive read-alouds in preschool and kindergarten. *The Reading Teacher, 60*(8), 742–751. https://doi.org/10.1598/RT.60.8.4

McNeill, K. L., & Krajeik, J. S. (2011). *Supporting grade 5–8 students in constructing explanations in science: The claim, evidence, and reasoning framework for talk and writing.* Pearson.

Milner, H. R. (2020). Disrupting racism and whiteness in researching a science of reading. *Reading Research Quarterly, 55*(S1), S249–S253. https://doi.org/10.1002/rrq.347

Mitchell, A. M., & Brady, S. A. (2013). The effect of vocabulary knowledge on novel word identification. *Ann. of Dyslexia 63*, 201–216. https://doi.org/10.1007/s11881-013-0080-1

Moje, E., Afflerbach, P., Enciso, P., & Lesaux, N. K. (2020). Game changers in reading research. In E. B. Moje, P. Afflerbach, P. Enciso, & N. K. Lesaux (Eds.), *Handbook of reading research* (Vol. 5, pp. 3–14). Routledge. https://doi.org/10.4324/9781315676302

Moll, L., Amanti, C., Neff, D., & Gonzalez, N. (1992). Funds of knowledge for teaching: Using qualitative approach to connect homes and classrooms. *Theory into Practice, 31*(2), 132–141.

Muhammad, G. (2020). *Cultivating genius: An equity framework for culturally and historically responsive literacy.* Scholastic.

Muhammad, G., Ortiz, N., & Neville, M. (2021). A historically responsive literacy model for reading and mathematics. *The Reading Teacher, 75*(1), 73–81. Retrieved online at: https://doi.org/10.1002/trtr.2035

Mulcahy, C. M. (2008). The tangled web we weave: Critical literacy and critical thinking. *Counterpoints, 326,* 15–27.

National Council of Teachers of English. (2018). *The students' right to read.* https://ncte.org/statement/righttoreadguideline/

National Council of Teachers of English. (2014). *NCTE's beliefs about students' right to write.* https://ncte.org/statement/students-right-to-write/

National Governors Association Center for Best Practices & Council of Chief State School Officers. (2010). *Common Core State Standards.* Author.

National Reading Panel. (2000). *Teaching children to read: An evidence-based assessment of the scientific research literature on reading and its implications for reading instruction* (National Institute of Health Pub. No. 00-4769). National Institute of Child Health and Human Development.

National Research Council. (2000). *How people learn: Brain, mind, experience, and school:* Expanded Edition. The National Academies Press. https://doi.org/10.17226/9853

New London Group (1996). A pedagogy of multiliteracies: Designing social futures. *Harvard Educational Review, 66*(1), 60–93.

NGSS Lead States. (2013). Next Generation Science Standards: For states, by states. The National Academies Press.

Nguyen, H. (2021). *5 ways to audit your classroom library for inclusion*. Edutopia. https://www.edutopia.org/article/5-ways-audit-your-classroom-library-inclusion

No Child Left Behind Act of 2001, Pub. L. No. 107–110, 20 U.S.C. § 6319 (2002).

Norris, S. P., & Phillips, L. M. (2012). Reading science: How a naive view of reading hinders so much else. In A. Zohar & Y. J. Dori (Eds.), *Metacognition in science education: Trends in current research* (pp. 37–56). Springer. http://doi.org/10.1007/978-94-007-2132-6_3

Osorio, S. (2020). Building culturally and linguistically sustaining spaces for emergent bilinguals: Using read-alouds to promote translanguaging. *The Reading Teacher, 74*(2), 127–135. https://doi.org/10.1002/trtr.1919

Ouellette, G. P. (2006). What's meaning got to do with it: The role of vocabulary in word reading and reading comprehension. *Journal of Educational Psychology, 98*(3), 554–566. https://doi.org/10.1037/0022-0663.98.3.554

Palincsar, A. S., Marcum, M. B., Fitzgerald, M., & Sherwood, C. A. (2019). Braiding teacher practice and class-wide dialogue: An historical inquiry across three sociocultural interventions. *International Journal of Educational Research, 97*, 157–165. https://doi.org/10.1016/j.ijer.2017.08.001

Park, S., Lee, S., Alonzo, M., & Adair, J. K. (2021). Reconceptualizing assistance for young children of color with disabilities in an inclusion classroom. *Topics in Early Childhood Special Education, 41*(1), 57–68. https://doi.org/10.1177/0271121421992429

Paugh, P. (2022). "I'm writing to teach those who do not know": Making the case for inclusive pedagogy that values difference and capitalizes on students' expertise. In D. Conrad & T. Abodeeb-Gentile (Eds.), *Intersections of diversity, literacy, and learner difficulties: Conversations between teacher, students and researchers.* Springer International.

Paugh, P. (2018). Trusting the students and each other: A story of critical collaborative praxis and critical literacy practice in an urban US classroom. *Interfaces Científicas-Educação, 7*(1), 37–46.

Paugh, P., & Moran, M. (2013). Growing language awareness in the classroom garden. *Language Arts, 90*(4), 253–267.

Paul, R., & Elder, L. (2005). *The thinker's guide to the nature and functions of critical & creative thinking.* Foundation for Critical Thinking.

Pearson, P. D. (2004). The reading wars. *Educational Policy, 18*(1), 216–252. https://doi.org/10.1177/0895904803260041

Perfetti, C. A., & Hart, L. (2002). The lexical quality hypothesis. In L. Vehoeven, C. Elbro, & P. Reitsma (Eds.), *Precursors of functional literacy* (pp. 189–213). John Benjamins.

Price, C. (2015). *Vitamania.* Penguin Press.

Ramachandra, V., Hewitt, L. E., & Brackenbury, T. (2011). The relationship between phonological memory, phonological sensitivity, and incidental word learning. *Journal of Psycholinguistic Research, 40*(2), 93–109. https://doi.org/10.1007/s10936-010-9157-8

Rastle, K. (2019). The place of morphology in learning to read in English. *Cortex, 116*, 45–54. https://doi.org/10.1016/j.cortex.2018.02.008

Reading Rockets. (n.d.). *Question–answer relationship (QAR).*

Reynolds, D., & Fisher, W. (2021). What happens when adolescents meet complex texts? Describing moments of scaffolding textual encounters. *Literacy.* https://doi.org/10.1111/lit.12258

Rigell, A., Banack, A., Maples, A., Laughter, J., Broemmel, A., Vines, N., & Jordan, J. (2022) Overwhelming whiteness: A critical analysis of race in a scripted reading curriculum, *Journal of Curriculum Studies*, 1–19. https://doi.org/10.1080/00220272.2022.2030803

Rose, D. (2011). Genre in the Sydney School. In J. Gee & M. Handford (eds.) *The Routledge Handbook of Discourse Analysis* (pp. 209–225). Routledge.

Rose, D., & Meyer, A. (2002). *Teaching every student in the digital age: Universal design for learning.* Association for Supervision and Curriculum Development.

Rosenblatt, L. M. (2018). The transactional theory of reading and writing. In D. E. Alvermann, N. J. Unrau, M. Sailors, & R. B. Ruddell (Eds.), *Theoretical models and processes of literacy* (pp. 451–479). Routledge.

Savage, R., Georgiou, G., Parrila, R., & Maiorino, K. (2018). Preventative reading interventions teaching direct mapping of graphemes in texts and set-for-variability aid at-risk learners. *Scientific Studies of Reading, 22*(3), 225–247. https://doi.org/10.1080/10888438.2018.1427753

Serafini, F. (2012). Reading multimodal texts in the 21st century. *Research in the Schools, 19*(1), 26–32.

Share, D. L. (1995). Phonological recoding and self teaching: Sine qua non of reading acquisition. *Cognition, 55*(2), 151–218. https://doi.org/10.1016/0010-0277(94)00645-2

Share, D. L. (2011). On the role of phonology in reading acquisition: The self-teaching hypothesis. In S. A. Brady, D. Braze, & C. A. Fowler (Eds.), *Explaining individual differences in reading: Theory and evidence* (pp. 45–68). Psychology Press.

Share, D. L. (2021). Is the science of reading just the science of reading English? *Reading Research Quarterly, 56*(S1), S391–S402. https://doi.org/10.1002/rrq.401

Shirley, D. (2021, July 5). Standardized testing is not the way forward: Schools should instead be focused on teaching and learning. *Commonwealth Magazine.* https://commonwealthmagazine.org/opinion/standardized-testing-is-not-the-way-forward/

Smolkin, L. B., & Donovan, C. A. (2003). Supporting comprehension acquisition for emerging and struggling readers: The interactive information book read-aloud. *Exceptionality, 11*(1), 25–38. https://doi.org/10.1207/S15327035EX1101_3

Snow, C., Burns, S., & Griffin, P. (Eds). (1998). *Preventing reading difficulties in young children.* National Academy Press.

Snow, C. E. (2018). Simple and not-so-simple views of reading. *Remedial and Special Education, 39*(5), 313–316. https://doi.org/10.1177/0741932518770288

Souto-Manning, M. (Ed.). (2020). *In the pursuit of justice: Students' rights to read and write in elementary school.* National Council of Teachers of English.

Souto-Manning, M., Ghim, H., & Madu, N. K. (2021). Toward early literacy as a site of belonging. *The Reading Teacher, 74*(5), 483–492. https://doi.org/10.1002/trtr.1992

Souto-Manning, M., & Rabadi-Raol, A. (2018). (Re)Centering quality in early childhood education: Toward intersectional justice for minoritized children. *Review of Research in Education, 42*(1), 203–225. https://doi.org/10.3102/0091732X18759550

Steacy, L. M., Wade-Woolley, L., Rueckl, J. G., Pugh, K. R., Elliott, J. D., & Compton, D. L. (2019). The role of set for variability in irregular word reading: Word and child predictors in typically developing readers and students at-risk for reading disabilities. *Scientific Studies of Reading, 23*(6), 523–532. https://doi.org/10.1080/10888438.2019.1620749

TED. (2009, October 7). *Chimamanda Ngozi Adichie: The danger of a single story* [Video]. YouTube. https://www.youtube.com/watch?v=D9Ihs241zeg

Thornton, N., & Osborne, A. (2022). A conversation with Drs. Gloria Boutte and April Baker-Bell. *Talking Points. 33*(2), 2-10.

Tortorelli, L. S., Lupo, S. M., & Wheatley, B. C. (2021). Examining teacher preparation for code-related reading instruction: An integrated literature review. *Reading Research Quarterly, 56*(S1), S317–S337. https://doi.org/10.1002/rrq.396

Tunmer, W. E., & Chapman, J. W. (2012). Does set for variability mediate the influence of vocabulary knowledge on the development of word recognition skills? *Scientific Studies of Reading, 16*(2), 122–140. https://doi.org/10.1080/10888438.2010.542527

Uccelli, P., Galloway, E. P., & Qin, W. (2020). The language for school literacy: Widening the lens on language and reading relations. In E. B. Moje, P. P. Afflerback, P. Enciso, N. K. Lesaux (Eds.), *Handbook of reading research* (Vol. 5, 155–179). Routledge.

United Nations Education, Scientific, & Cultural Organization (UNESCO). (2014). *Global citizenship: Preparing learners for the challenges of the 21st century* [report, p. 9]. Retrieved online: https://unesdoc.unesco.org/ark:/48223/pf0000227729

Valencia, S. W., Place, N. A., Martin, S. D., & Grossman, P. L. (2006). Curriculum materials for elementary reading: Shackles and scaffolds for four beginning teachers. *The Elementary School Journal, 107*(1), 93–120. https://doi.org/10.1086/509528

Van den Broek, P., Lorch, R. F., Linderholm, T., & Gustafson, M. (2001). The effects of readers' goals on inference generation and memory for texts. *Memory & Cognition, 29*(8), 1081–1087. https://doi.org/10.3758/BF03206376

Vasquez, V. M. (2004). *Negotiating critical literacies with young children.* Earlbaum.

Vasquez, V. M., Janks, H., & Comber, B. (2019). Critical literacy as a way of being and doing. *Language Arts, 96*(5), 300–311.

Venezky, R. L. (1999). *The American way of spelling: The structure and origins of American English orthography.* Guilford Press.

Wagner, R. K., & Torgesen, J. K. (1987). The nature of phonological processing and its causal role in the acquisition of reading skills. *Psychological Bulletin, 101*(2), 192–212. https://doi.org/10.1037/0033-2909.101.2.192

Waitoller, F., &. Thorius, K. (2016). Cross-pollinating culturally sustaining pedagogy and universal design for learning: Toward an inclusive pedagogy that accounts for Dis/ability. *Harvard Education Review, 6*(3), 366–390. https://doi.org/10.17763/1943-5045-86.3.366

Wesche, M. B., & Paribakht, T. S. (1996). Assessing second language vocabulary knowledge: Depth versus breadth. *Canadian Modern Language Review, 53*(1), 13–40. https://doi.org/10.3138/cmlr.53.1.13

WIDA. (2020). *WIDA English language development standards framework, 2020 edition: Kindergarten–grade 12.* Board of Regents of the University of Wisconsin System.

Willis, A. I. (2019). Race, response to intervention, and reading research. *Journal of Literacy Research, 51*(4), 394–419. https://doi.org/10.1177/1086296X19877463

Woulfin, S. L., & Gabriel, R. E. (2020). Interconnected infrastructure for improving reading instruction. *Reading Research Quarterly, 55*(S1), S109–S117. https://doi.org/10.1002/rrq.339

Wright, T. S. (2018/2019). Reading to learn from the start: The power of interactive read alouds. *American Educator, 42*(2), 4–8, 40.

Wright, T. S., & Neuman, S. B. (2014). Paucity and disparity in kindergarten oral vocabulary instruction. *Journal of Literacy Research, 46*(3), 330–357. https://doi.org/10.1177/1086296X14551474

Zhang, S., & Duke, N. K. (2008). Strategies for internet reading with different reading purposes: A descriptive study of twelve good internet readers. *Journal of Literacy Research, 40*(1), 128–162. https://doi.org/10.1080/10862960802070491

Zipke, M. (2016). The importance of flexibility of pronunciation in learning to decode: A training study in set for variability. *First Language, 36*(1), 71–86. https://doi.org/10.1177/0142723716639495

Zucker, T. A., Cabell, S. Q., & Pico, D. L. (2021). Going nuts for words: Recommendations for teaching young students academic vocabulary. *The Reading Teacher, 74*(5), 581–594. https://doi.org/10.1002/trtr.1967

CHILDREN'S BOOK REFERENCES

Ada, A. F. (1999/2002). *I love Saturdays y domingos.* Atheneum Books for Young Readers.

Agra-Deedy, C. (2017). *The rooster who would not be quiet.* Scholastic Press.

Al-Abdullah, R. (2010). *The sandwich swap.* Disney-Hyperion Books.

Choi, Y. (2003). *The name jar.* Firefly Books.

Cronin, D., & Lewin, B., (2000). *Click, clack, moo: Cows that type.* Simon & Schuster.

D'Aluisio, F., & Menzel, P. (2008) *What the world eats.* Tricycle Press.

Diaz, Junot (2018). *Island born.* Penguin.

Holman, S. (1998). *Grandpa, is everything Black bad?* Culture Coop.

Layton, N. (2019). *A planet full of plastic.* Hachette Children's Group.

Lin, G. (2018). *A big mooncake for little star.* Little, Brown Books.

Morales, Y. (2018). *Dreamers.* Holiday House Books.

Paul, M. (2015). *One plastic bag: Isatou Ceesay and the recycling women of the Gambia.* Milbrook Press.

Penfold, A. (2018). *All are welcome.* Knopf Books for Young Readers.

Yousafzi, M. (2017). *Malala's magic pencil.* Little Brown and Company.

Index

"breaking the code"
  described, 22
Brisk, M. E., 41–42
broad range of research
  necessity of, 119
"building blocks"
  meaning units as, 37
building competence and confi-
    dence, 77–94
  case example, 78–79
  cognition/emotion relationship
    in, 80–84
  in literacy education, 125
  rethinking current school prac-
    tices to affirm positive literacy
    identities in, 88–94
  shifting toward asset-oriented
    pedagogies in, 84–88

Cabell, S. Q., 63
"Can Do Philosophy," 49
Cartwright, K. B., 48, 52
CCBC. see Cooperative Children's
    Book Center (CCBC)
CCSS. see Common Core State Stan-
    dards (CCSS)
Cervetti, G. N., 123–26
Chall, J. S., xxiii
children's literature
  awards for, 108, 109t
choice
  benefits of, xxvi–xxvii
clarifier(s)
  in reciprocal teaching, 75
classroom talk
  deep connections with meaning-
    ful texts related to, 59–60

clause(s)
  complex, 47t
  dependent, 47t
  independent, 47t
Click, Clack, Moo, 96–97
close reading, 103–4
  defined, 98
  described, 74
  tools for, 104
Cochran-Smith, M., 129
code(s)
  "breaking" of, 22
  language. see language code(s)
  learning of, xvi, xvif, 16, 16f, 22–50.
      see also learning the codes
  word-level, 28–40, 30t, 32t–33t, 39t.
      see also word-level codes
"code-switching," 93
coding competence
  in four resources model, 18–19
cognate(s), 40
cognition
  emotion and, 80–84
cognitive ability
  literacy learning as, xvii
cognitive development
  confidence in shaping, 78
  contextual (social) experiences
    in framing, 81
  social context and, 7
cognitive growth
  literacy teaching and, xvii
"College and Career Readiness," 10
Colorin Colorado
  critical literacy resources offered
    by, 110t
Comber, B., 105

About the Authors

Patricia Paugh is a professor in the College of Education and Human Development at the University of Massachusetts Boston, where she teaches literacy methods courses and is graduate program director for elementary education. Pat's scholarship is centered on issues of critical and disciplinary literacy in early childhood and elementary education primarily through collaborative research with teachers in urban classrooms. Her work has been published in academic and professional journals including: *Language Arts, Journal of Literacy Research, Reading Research Quarterly, Literacy Researcher: Theory, Method, Practice*, and *Teaching Education*. She has also published three coedited volumes focused on literacy learning. Pat brings an extensive background as a first grade teacher and elementary reading specialist to her current practice as a teacher educator in a public university and as an advocate for teachers' professionalism.

Deborah MacPhee is a professor in the School of Teaching and Learning at Illinois State University in Normal, Illinois, where she teaches literacy methods courses for undergraduates and directs the Mary and Jean Borg Center for Reading and Literacy. Deborah's research critically examines discourses of literacy coaching and professional development school interactions and metaphors used in media portrayals of the science of reading. Her work has been published in several academic and professional journals, including *Reading Research Quarterly, The Reading Teacher, The International Journal of Mentoring and Coaching in Education, School-University Partnerships*, and *The New Educator*. Deborah is a former first- and second-grade teacher who currently assesses and tutors students who experience difficulty learning to read.